For Stephanie
May all your
dreams come
true

Jean Bryant
5-10-86

ANY-BODY CAN WRITE

A Playful Approach

JEAN BRYANT

Whatever Publishing, Inc.
Mill Valley, California

Published by Whatever Publishing, Inc.
P.O. Box 137, Mill Valley, CA 94942

Cover by Kathleen Vande Kieft

ISBN 0-931432-21-9

For Barbara Large,
who believed in me until I could believe in myself,
and to all my students,
who taught me about the process of writing.

CONTENTS

PART THREE: EVERYBODY HAS DIFFICULTIES

PART FOUR: ANYBODY CAN KEEP WRITING

About Magic

People come to my workshops wanting *magic:* a secret formula for getting words on paper, for telling their stories, for realizing success in their writing.

I tell them, "There *is* no magic!"

I do know that *anybody can write*, and that self-acceptance, self-knowledge, and belief in oneself are necessary to begin the struggle with words on paper. And I know it takes both trust and courage to continue that struggle.

I also know that writing is personally valuable, and that the act of writing is life-enhancing and pleasurable, an outlet for creativity.

No one *needs* a writing workshop, or a teacher, or another how-to-write book. No one needs magic to do it.

The paradox is that when you give up the illusion of magic and settle down to work, to play with words on paper, to write regularly, *magic* often occurs!

In this book, and in my classes and workshops, I seek to help people get from where they are now to where they want to go — with their ideas, their stories, their dreams of writing. I want to help turn wishful thinking into successful doing, to turn you on to the joy of writing, the experience of writing, the *magic* of *you* as writer!

PART ONE

ANYBODY CAN DREAM

1

The Dream Began When...

When I was a pigtailed eight-and-a-half, I checked out a marvelous old book from the Santa Fe Public Library on how to make things out of paper. "All you need," it began, "is paper, scissors, and a little gumption."

I raced into the kitchen looking for my mother. I found her weeding hollyhocks on the patio outdoors.

"Mommy, do we have any gumption?" I asked, thinking it must be something like glue or mucilage. Laughing, she referred me to the heavy *Webster's Unabridged* in the bookcase. I read:

gump-tion (gump shun), n. Informal
1. *initiative; aggressiveness; resourcefulness*
2. *courage; spunk; guts*

It turned out gumption was something I already had, though I didn't know it. That story often comes to mind when I work with someone who wants to write. I tell it to the hesitant ones, the fearful ones, those who feel like they can't write — for whatever reason.

All you need if you want to write is paper, pen or pencil, and a little gumption.

You don't need a fancy education or super intelligence. You don't need to know how to spell, or punctuate, or cipher, or improve your vocabulary in only thirty days.

All you need, if you want to write, is experience: experience in writing and experience in living. The life experience you already have. The writing experience comes from the willingness to put words on paper, to be honest in your writing, and to learn from doing it.

Willingness, gumption, and maybe some encouragement. If you have willingness and gumption, the encouragement will follow.

Ability to write, like gumption, is not something you have to get, but something you already have, although you may not know it yet. Anybody *can* do it. *Anybody can write.*

Skeptic or believer, you wouldn't be reading this book at all if you didn't hope that "anybody" might mean you too. Those who possess curiosity, a little gumption, and the dream of being a writer will be open to learning, and succeeding at writing.

My dream of being a writer really started the day I learned to read in the first grade. Reading unlocked a whole exciting world of happiness through vicarious experience. The joy of reading sparked the beginning of my haphazard education in the libraries of the west. Book-learning challenged and delighted me.

School-learning disappointed and disillusioned me. I hated being told what to do, hated having to read dumb and boring stuff, and I especially hated having to write. My painful shyness and oversensitivity didn't help. My family moved a lot; I attended nine schools in twelve years. My grades varied: some Fs, a few As. "Working below ability" felt like high praise on my report cards.

No one ever called me a good student. But in retrospect

I realize I was a good learner: I was always reading (although seldom reading what I was supposed to). But I managed to avoid writing, and usually squeaked by on multiple-choice tests; multiple-guess would be more accurate.

Not a good student, but definitely a good learner. Learning things about myself rather than about school subjects. Learning that I never did anything right, or at least right enough to please my teachers. Learning that I was "lazy," that I was uncreative, that I didn't measure up.

One day, during third-grade art, we finally got to use the tempera paints. Many cautions about "being neat" accompanied a big swatch of blank newsprint for each of us.

"You can paint whatever you like," the teacher said.

Looking at all the colors, my excitement grew. I wanted to try every one. First, I daubed some red onto the paper. Then spatters of orange, globs of purple. Splendid! A smooth glow of yellow, wispy lines of brown. Magic! Caught up in the doing, the process, I didn't hear the teacher until she stood right beside me.

"What is it?" she asked.

I thought a minute.

"A flower garden?" My voice wavered, seeking approval.

She grabbed the brush out of my hand, rinsed it briskly, dipped it into the green jar, and executed a bold series of strokes across the page. My page!

"This is what you want to do," she said, and continued on to "help" the next unsuspecting student.

My stomach hurt. I looked at how she'd messed up my painting, by showing me what *I* wanted to do. My idea, my fun — ruined! I wanted to rip the paper off the easel, wad it up, and stomp on it. But I supposed she must be right, and I dutifully completed it, but the magic of the doing had disappeared.

At the end of the week we had to take the paintings

home. My mother loved the picture. Raved about it. Said how remarkable it was "for a child my age." I tried to explain how the teacher had "helped," that it really wasn't my work, and that the good part was the teacher's.

She didn't really understand. She had the damn thing framed to hang in the living room. I always felt funny about it, especially when she bragged about it to her friends. I knew it wasn't really my work. I knew I hadn't done it right!

My teachers always said writing, in particular, needed to be done right. Writing should be organized. Writers needed to be disciplined. But I'd already learned that I was lazy, that I had a bad attitude. "Stop daydreaming," they said, so I learned to hide *Arabian Nights* behind my grammar book. I learned not to get caught.

They said writers needed to have talent. No one ever accused me of having talent, except a talent for wasting time.

"You shouldn't read so much. You need fresh air," my mother said.

So, in the summertime, I hauled an armload of books outdoors into the backyard treehouse. In the winter, I hid in my closet with a flashlight, a pillow, and a book.

"Good girls don't tell stories," they said, which meant "don't exaggerate" or "stop lying." So, I learned to be silent. And sullen. I learned very well all the things I wasn't. I learned to feel inadequate, unworthy, uncreative. I learned how to get through high school without doing any writing to speak of.

Nevertheless, the dream of being a writer "someday" never died. I read every how-to-write book I could find, as well as biographies of authors and books on writing techniques. But I never picked up a pencil to write a word. The sight of a blank sheet of paper always intimidated me and discouraged me from trying.

I started college, dropped out, and drifted into an early marriage and motherhood, still daydreaming about being a writer. I remained a functional half-literate until the age of twenty-seven: speaking only when spoken to, thinking up a lot of ideas for stories, reading omnivorously, but writing nothing — not even letters to my mother.

Finally, I signed up for a twice-weekly adult education class called Creative Writing. I'd been out of school for ten years, had four children under the age of five, and desperately needed to get out of the house two nights a week.

Lucky me! The teacher loved writing and loved teaching. Her excitement, her belief that all of us could write, fired my imagination. My hopes began to rise. Her enthusiasm was contagious. I kept taking and retaking the class. I learned about writing, but more importantly, I learned about myself. The subject of writing ended up being less important than the impact and caring of the teacher. If she had taught Differential Calculus, I would have signed up for it.

The major reason I lead workshops today, and have written this book, is to pass on to others what she gave to me: a sense of excitement about writing and language, a sense of joy in the act of writing and the expression of one's ideas in words. A belief in the value of personal experience and the value of pouring it onto paper. A profound trust in the self, and a glorious sense of possibility, resulting from playing with words on paper. In short, all the pleasures and rewards of a writing life.

2

Who Is Anybody?

When I get a new book, especially a how-to book, my approach is tentative, curious. I want to get a sense of it and the author, want to sniff it out, become a little familiar with it and get acquainted before settling down to read. First I glance at the table of contents, scan the front and back covers, and page through it rapidly to see if anything engages my interest. When seriously ready to read, I may begin with a section in the middle. Then I go back to the beginning. And, if the book engages me, I'll read it all the way through.

How-to books often have exercises, things to do which must be done in sequence before you may turn the page. Those do-not-read-further injunctions always frustrate me. Sometimes I read on anyway, and then feel like I've blown it. Often I stop reading altogether and mark my place, with good intentions to do the exercise (especially if it sounds interesting) before continuing. Occasionally it takes me a long time to get back to the book.

Books offend me when they offer good ideas and information but don't give me credit for knowing how best to use them for myself. Therefore: *I trust you to know how to use this book for yourself, or to be able to figure it out.*

There's no wrong way to use this book. Equally important, there's no right way to use it either. I'd be delighted if you found it so engaging, so interesting, that you read it straight through and did all the suggested *Wordplay* and *Writing Experiences* as you encountered them. And, in that process, you got turned onto writing and onto yourself as a person who writes.

But I might be even more pleased if you opened it up to a section you were curious about now. One starting point is just as good as another. Do the writing parts when you're "good and ready." Or never at all, if that's what suits you.

I'm a rebel. I don't like following directions. School and teachers and all the other grownups of the world told me that was bad. For a long time, I believed them. Now I believe that a dislike for arbitrary, this-is-the-only-way-to-do-it directions can be a sign of creativity in action. Trust your intuition about what's good for you. Trust your creativity in action.

In my workshops, when it's time to write, I'll say, "Do this. I'll be watching." I make the request and set aside class time for writing. The group agrees to do it, thereby supporting each other in following my directions.

All I can do in this book is to suggest and encourage, in hopes that you will be intrigued enough and challenged enough to try the suggestions. To try one...and another...and then another.

The ideas for writing presented here are simple, very easy to do. However, their simplicity is deceptive. They will work best if you're willing to have fun with them, to approach them with a spirit of playfulness. If you're open to having a deeper experience with them, that will happen more readily if you do them "just for fun."

No matter how sophisticated or educated you are, the

ideas will have value for you *if you do them*. If you're not quite ready yet to try writing, perhaps this book will help you to be ready soon, to be somebody who can write.

The title for this book came from a student who took one of my Beginning Writing workshops. At the end of the six-hour day, she raised her hand. Her face glowed with accomplishment.

"When I came in here this morning," she said, "I didn't believe I could write. But somehow, you've convinced me I can. Look." She held up her spiral notebook with dozens of hand-scrawled pages. "You know what you should call this class?" she asked me.

"What?" I asked. "Anybody can write," she said. "Anybody can write."

Well, I know a good title when I hear one and I began using it.

In my workshops, there's a spontaneity in the structure. I put together each workshop as we go along, getting acquainted with the particular needs of each group of students. I bring along a book-bag of materials: notes, ideas for writing, quotes, books, and my own lively self, but I use my experiences and those of my former students as my primary resource.

This book is intended to function like a self-guided workshop for you.

I wish I could see you, and sit and talk with you face to face. I wish I could hear you talk, and respond to your questions, your enthusiasms, your uncertainties about writing. I'd like to be able to see when I was boring you, or making things too difficult. When I was explaining too much, or not enough. To see you gazing out the window, or starting to daydream. To watch your foot swinging, or hear the pencil tapping or paper shuffling that indicates you're losing interest.

I want to share my lifelong love affair with words on

paper. To share my love of books, the look and the smell and the feel of them. To share my love of writing itself, of the pencil in my hand and the stringing out of the words onto the smooth face of the paper.

I also want to share my fascination with people, with their desire to write and the difficulties they encounter in trying to do it. I'd like to share my delight in seeing them get absorbed in the process of exploring their many selves on paper.

When we're children, the world of books and reading (television, too, nowadays) opens up a whole new world — the outer world. It's a place to learn about other people. In learning about others, we understand ourselves more. Similarly, the world of writing opens up a different new world, the inner world, where learning about ourselves gives us knowledge about others. That knowledge gives us compassion, and power.

Writing is a way to use everything that has ever happened to you in a positive and creative way. Whether you want to write because you have ideas, or whether you want to write for your family, or even for magazines, it all starts with putting words on paper. There will be a lot of words in the beginning!

My students are people like myself who never totally gave up the hope or the dream of being a writer. Many are also people like me who never did well in school, or who may feel uneducated, or uneducable. Some of my students are people who feel overeducated — stifled by all the rules or afflicted with perfectionism. Many of them are convinced that they lack creativity, talent, or originality. They compare themselves with great writers, or with their friends, and judge themselves inadequate.

In the last dozen years, I've worked with thousands of writers or would-be writers. Many of my students are very intelligent. Some are multi-degreed professionals, educated people who want to write but don't feel any more confident of their ability than those like me with less formal education. The common denominator is the dream of being a writer.

Dreaming of being a writer, however, is not writing. Thinking about writing is not writing. Getting excited by ideas for stories, plotting out a book in your head, reading about writing: none of these is writing.

Writing is putting words on paper, first one sentence and then another. Or even one word and then another.

What often happens is that people try, but get discouraged before they've barely started. People need to get *un*discouraged. They need courage to begin, and to keep going. They need to understand what the writing process is, to understand what happens physically, mentally, and emotionally when they sit down to write.

3

Education, Einstein, and Creativity

A s children we are both curious and highly creative. We explore, touching everything we can get our hands on. We ask "why?" about everything. We don't know how things should be done, so we try it one way, then another, learning as we go — until some well-meaning parent or teacher interferes.

Creative people, of whatever age, have certain things in common. They challenge assumptions. They recognize patterns and see in new ways. They make connections and construct networks. They take advantage of chance. Nothing is wasted. Mistakes are used. Most important of all, they take risks. They dare to say, "So it hasn't been done before, or it hasn't been done that way before, or 'they' say it can't be done at all. So what?"

This approach to life and learning is usually stifled and ultimately destroyed by traditional education. Tradition is based on precedent. *This is the way we do it. This is the way it's always been done.* Public education, according to Alvin Toffler in *The Third Wave*, was an outgrowth of the industrial

21

revolution, of the need to produce good, well-conditioned factory workers.

Therefore, besides the overt curriculum of the three Rs — reading, writing, arithmetic — there was, according to Toffler, a subtle and pervasive "covert curriculum of punctuality, obedience, and rote-repetitive work."[1] Those learning experiences prepared people to be good factory workers, but also discouraged innovation, spontaneity, creativity, and independent thinking. Creativity was not only discouraged, but also punished.

Albert Einstein recalled his relief at ending his formal education:

> *It is, in fact, nothing short of a miracle that the modern methods of instruction have not yet entirely strangled the holy curiosity of inquiry, for this delicate little plant, aside from stimulation, stands mostly in need of freedom; without this it goes to wreck and ruin without fail. It is a very grave mistake to think that the enjoyment of* seeing *and* searching *can be promoted by means of coercion and a sense of duty.*[2]

Highly educated people, perhaps with several university degrees, will often follow more elaborate and complex sets of rules for doing any and every thing, especially writing. It's not that grammar and a sense of order in language aren't useful. It's just that they are often misunderstood and applied inappropriately. Following inappropriate rules in writing can seriously interfere with creativity. *The fear of being wrong is the prime inhibitor of the creative process.*

Pearl Buck, a serious novelist and popular writer, understood the source of creativity. She said:

> *The truly creative mind in any field is no more than this: a human creature born abnormally, inhumanly sensitive. To him a touch is a blow, a sound is a noise, a misfortune is a tragedy, a joy is an ecstasy, a friend is a lover, a lover is a god, and failure is death. Add to this*

cruelly delicate organism the overpowering necessity to create, create, create — so that without the creating of music or poetry or books or buildings or something of meaning, his very breath is cut off from him. He must create, must pour out creation. By some strange, un- known, inward urgency, he is not really alive unless he is creating.[3]

4

The Joy of Unlearning

Writing skill, creativity of expression, and even talent, I ultimately learned, come not from formal education, but from one's own struggles with words on paper. From pouring out creation, as Pearl Buck said.

We're often unable to engage in that struggle, however, until we do some unlearning. Not only unlearning grammar, spelling, and punctuation rules, but also unlearning things we've assimilated from our reading, from peers and grown-ups, and from assumptions provided by our own critical faculties. We need to examine our assumptions about good writing versus bad writing.

In addition, we need to unlearn things we've learned about ourselves, especially about expressing ourselves. About whether we think we're creative or talented, what we think we can or can't do, who we think we are or aren't. About politeness versus honesty, and about our intelligence, our personality, our achievement.

Whether or not we've ever thought of ourselves as good students, we are all good learners.

The first task in my workshops is to help people get

unhooked from all the education they've had. Once they've begun to do that, the real learning begins. Often, it begins with a challenge. I make a controversial statement, such as "Thinking isn't useful in the first stage of writing."

A hand goes up.

"I don't understand what you said," or "I don't believe that," someone says. "Prove it."

"What's *your* experience?" I ask. Or "Prove it for yourself," I challenge back.

Those students always question. They make waves. They don't always follow my advice (and, of course, I give excellent advice). They are not good students, but they want to learn, and that's more important than anything.

The students I appreciate the most are the ones who tend to be skeptical, the ones who demand value. Once these students understand that all there is to writing is *doing it*, they are often willing to engage in the trial-and-error-and-error-and-error learning process. They are also often willing to begin to trust themselves and their own experience.

I'm convinced that each one of us knows best not only what to write, but also how to accomplish it, much better than anyone else can. Sometimes I give assignments or suggestions for writing exercises, but I like it better when students don't do them, and instead use their time to write something they feel strongly about. To trust themselves not only to write it, but also to share it with the class.

Back in my first writing class, I had no trust in myself, my writing, or my creativity. I did think I had two things going for me: (1) a large vocabulary — all those glorious multi-syllabled words I had learned, and (2) techniques I'd picked up from reading all the how-to-write books in the library.

But I was wrong on both counts. My greatest liabilities, and the first things I had to give up, were my inappropriate vocabulary and my know-it-all attitude about technique.

Only after painfully unlearning what I thought I knew about good writing, only after I gave up showing off my high-powered vocabulary, did my writing begin to improve and come alive.

I'd drive home from class revved up, stimulated by what I'd heard. Ideas bloomed grand and magnificent in my head. I couldn't wait to get home and begin writing. I'd start to write, wrestling with my idea. I'd keep at it doggedly, become frustrated, and stop. Then I'd work at it some more, struggling to improve it. Then I'd read it over before the next class. It was terrible, horrible, awful! What had happened to my exciting ideas? They were dead! Somehow, I'd killed them. Reluctantly, I'd drag them to class. And I'd cringe when they were read aloud. Paper rustling and faint snoring confirmed my negative assessment.

I was disappointed. Disillusioned. Discouraged. I remembered I wasn't talented or creative. I didn't have anything to write about, anyway. I wasn't interesting and neither was my life. What happened to me on paper was equally uninteresting. It was dull. It was boring. Everybody else did better than I did. Dreaming of being a writer all those years had felt exciting and romantic. The reality was awful.

But the teacher didn't give up on me. She encouraged me to continue. So, despite the agony of putting words on paper, each word like a drop of my life's blood, I persevered.

I persevered primarily out of a dire need to communicate, because shyness restricted me verbally. I also kept at it because somebody else (the teacher) thought I could do it despite my ineptness, despite my handicaps.

Within two years, I'd completed and sold a few pieces to my local newspaper. Of course, I started many more than I ever completed. Writing still was difficult, still painful, but the rewards of reaching an audience kept me at it. My first fan letter began with the word "Horsefeathers" and was unsigned. I was delighted. I didn't care that the reader thought I was an idiot. I knew my work needed lots of improvement. My delight sprang from the fact that not only had it been published, but that someone had read it and *reacted*. Even better, the greater joys of writing for self-discovery began to pay off in unexpected ways.

Your reaction to what you've read so far is important. Do you have a sense of some of the things you've learned about yourself and about writing that might have interfered with your dreams of writing?

The ideas presented here offer you a chance to start fresh, to begin putting words on paper, and to improve your relationship with the act of writing. You can learn to enjoy the process of expressing yourself with the written word. But let's get rid of some old "stuff" first.

WORDPLAY #1

Dump out on paper a list of the unuseful things you've learned about writing. Add any discouraging experiences you've had with writing up to this point. Don't forget to jot down some of your bad habits and personality traits. This list doesn't have to be exhaustive or organized in any way — take just five to ten minutes to do it. (At this point, you might prefer to do it mentally, or just read on through.)

Examples:

"can't spell"

"my Dad says I'm too lazy"

"not good grammar"

"I hate typing and my handwriting is illegible"

"no original ideas"

"too much like work"

"I always got Ds in English"

"my cousin is a reporter and smarter than me"

"if I can't do it perfect what's the use?"
"everything is dull and boring"
"I think I'm probably too lazy"
"writing is just too hard"
"I think too fast — can't slow my head down"
"Miss Smith in eighth grade read my paper as an example of what not to do!"
"I start things and never finish them"
"writing is too much like school"
"can't never do anything right anyway"
"I never like anything I write"

This will give you a sense of what we're after. Don't spend too much time on it. Just scrawl a few notes, and then put it aside for a moment. I want to tell you a story.

In Santa Fe, New Mexico, every Labor Day weekend there's a big, three-day fiesta. I have childhood memories of the carnival spirit, the drunken brawls in the plaza, the religious candlelight procession, and much dancing and eating. What I really looked forward to, however, was the finale of the celebration — the burning of Zozobra or "Old Man Gloom."

Zozobra caught my imagination and has held it all these years. He was a grotesque figure, maybe thirty feet tall, constructed of wire and sticks like a giant marionette, and he grinned horribly down at the gathering crowd. People drifted toward the municipal baseball field at dusk to witness the burning of Old Man Gloom. Great groans and shrieks over the loudspeaker intensified as smoke and flames curled around the effigy. Zozobra writhed and twisted, then finally died as the fireworks display began. Cleansed and purged, we danced while crimson and amber starbursts rained down on us.

The Southwesterners believed the Zozobra personified

all their unhappiness and the wrongs of the past year. Therefore, all the gloomy stuff, all their sorrows and difficulties, died with the end of summer. Every fall was a fresh slate — a new beginning.

WORDPLAY #2

Take a new piece of paper and using the items on the list you just made, construct or sketch with your words or phrases a stick figure, an Old Man Gloom to represent your bad feelings or negative experiences with writing. Here's an example:

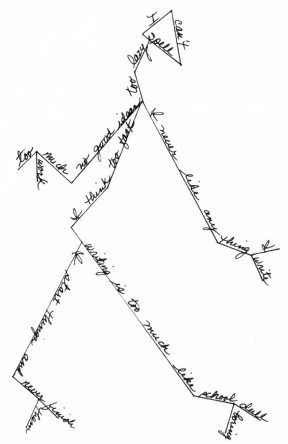

After you finish filling in the stick figure with your own phrases, you can then tear it into small pieces and burn it in an ashtray or throw it into the fireplace; or simply make a paper airplane out of it and sail it away. Tie it to a helium balloon and release it (and all of your other "old business" with writing) to float away into the sky. You may even think of a better way!

Now you have a fresh slate — a new beginning.

5

Doing Versus Dreaming

L et's look at some of the different aspects or tasks con-
nected with writing, or dreaming of being a writer.
Here are some that appeal to me:

Thinking up ideas. Jotting ideas on the backs of enve-
lopes. Reading books, including books on writing. Making
lists of things to write articles or stories or books about...
someday. Taking classes on grammar, vocabulary, spelling
and composition, as well as writers' workshops. Beginning
notes for a novel. Writing in a journal. Talking about writing.
Going to a writers' conference, and listening to the experts
discuss writing and getting published.

Dreaming up stories. Wishing for the time to write
more. Thinking about writing better. Writing letters. Shuffling papers on my desk. Researching. Sharpening my pencil. Writing regularly. Rewriting and rewriting some more.
Looking up facts in the almanac; looking through *Bartlett's
Quotations*. Creating analogies. Interviewing experts. Phon-
ing the information lady at the public library. Writing memos
on the job. Writing papers for school. Writing poems. Typing
a full manuscript.

WORDPLAY #3

Now take out a piece of paper and construct a list of activities that you associate with writing. You probably can add some different or more specific ones to your list. And some of the ones I've listed may not apply to you at all.

How can you tell how much of what you're doing really is productive writing, and how much is thinking or dreaming? The next *Wordplay* will show you how to use your list of writing activities to figure out how you're spending your time in relationship to writing.

WORDPLAY #4

1. Take out a sheet of paper and section it off in a grid as in the following illustration.

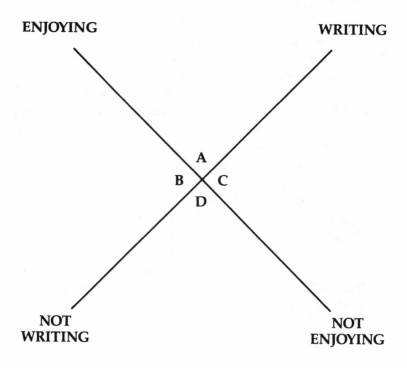

2. You'll notice there are four categories listed on the grid. Here are the guidelines for filling in each category:

In section A, *Enjoying Writing*, list all the activities that give your experience the quality of joy, delight, satisfaction, or accomplishment, as in "I'm doing it and I feel good about it."

In section B, *Enjoying Not-writing*, list those items that involve thinking about writing: dreaming, fantasizing or goal-setting, as in "I'm not doing that much, but it's fun to daydream."

In section C, *Not-enjoying Writing*, the quality of experience is drudgery or compulsion — "I have to do it, but I don't like it."

In section D, *Not enjoying Not-writing*, the quality of experience is duty or guilt — "I should be doing it, but I'm not doing it, and feel guilty because I'm not."

3. Take five to fifteen minutes to pencil in the four sections with items from your list. Some of your items may belong in more than one section. If so, see if you can figure out how to break them down into smaller parts. For instance, I may enjoy taking classes, but hate doing assignments. I may enjoy reading books on writing, but feel guilty if I'm not actually writing. I may enjoy writing a story, but when I reread it I don't like the way it turned out.

After you're through filling in the sections, look to see where most of your involvement with writing occurs. *Caution:* this exercise is just for your information and is not intended to make you feel bad (or good). Play around with this way of looking at your involvement with writing.

Here's what my chart looked like during my first ten years of writing:

ENJOYING   WRITING

Taking classes. Reading books. Doing research. Writing memos. Thinking up ideas. Talking about writing. Dreaming up stories. Going to writers' conferences. Thinking about writing.

Writing in a journal. Jotting down ideas. Writing poetry.

Writing letters. Rewriting. Doing class assignments. Struggling through first drafts.

A

B

C

D

Feeling guilty for not writing. Feeling guilty about missed deadlines. Feeling envious of my classmates' successful writing. Neglecting to answer letters.

NOT WRITING   NOT ENJOYING

For much of my writing life, most of what I did fell into sections B, C, and D. I still dabble around in those sections. However, more and more of my experience with writing is enjoyable and oriented toward action and results (section A). And I encourage myself and my students to study and work with our involvement in order to move more of our energy into delight, and active writing, putting words on paper with active enjoyment.

For me, that means making friends with my typewriter, and not talking out my stories before I get them on paper. And it means either finishing what I start or not feeling guilty when I don't complete my ideas. It means withholding judgment until my first raggedy draft is spilled out onto paper from beginning to end. It means improving my grammar and/or vocabulary by more involvement with the *act* of writing rather than memorizing abstract grammatical rules out of context. And realizing that all will often improve spontaneously if I just do a lot more writing. Over the years, not surprisingly, my success in writing has been in direct proportion to the amount of time I put in at my desk.

I want to feel good about my writing, about my involvement with writing. The better I feel about it, the more likely I am to do more of it, and then I'll feel even better about being productive. I don't want to spend too much time in activities I dislike, and I don't like the guilt that keeps company with the word "should." The important thing to know about this word is that every "should" has a kernel of truth and a kernel of a lie, equally balanced. Probing beneath the surface to isolate that grain of truth and that hidden lie can lead to freedom from guilt.

Consider this example: I *should* write more. The truth: I have both the time and the energy to do it. The lie: it's important for me to write more. (It's obviously not important *enough* in my life right now to use that time and energy on writing. Results do determine intentions.)

The passive enjoyment of section B can become an energy drain, leading to the frustration of living a life of wishful thinking without the satisfaction of real accomplishment. Doing or dreaming, it's up to you. What do you want to experience?

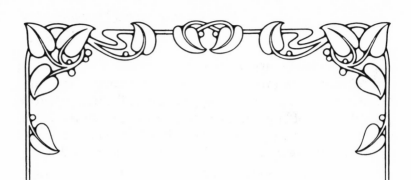

EXPERIENCE IS THE REAL TEACHER

Experience is the Real *teacher* —
Experience in writing — and experience in living —
Life experiences you already have.

Writing experience comes from willingness:
to surrender to an idea
to grab that pencil
to begin scribbling away

To act like a lightning rod in a BRAINSTORM

To fingerpaint with words on paper

Willingness to keep playing with the idea:
Until — it comes ALIVE!

Until — that vital connection between it and
your uniqueness happens

Until — it Surpr!zez the Hell out of you!

PART TWO

ANYBODY CAN WRITE

6

Beliefs, Myths, Illusions

"I don't have writer's block. Writing is just something I can't do."

I often hear this statement in my workshops. Many of my students believe they simply can't write, or at least not well.

Beliefs are one of the important sources of knowledge about the world. They come from our upbringing, education, or religion, and they affect the ways we live and behave. Beliefs can widen our world or restrict our experience. They can keep us from appreciating our own uniqueness, and sometimes they even keep us from experiencing pleasure or satisfaction in what we're doing.

One of the major limiting beliefs about writing is that if you're writing, or if you have a desire to write, then you must have a definite goal; writing for publication is presumed to be the highest or most desirable goal. Writing for fun, for friends or family, or just for yourself may seem frivolous to others. Letters or storytelling for children are vaguely acceptable, but certainly no match for the prestige of published writing.

If you confess to writing for self-expression or for pleasure, it sounds self-indulgent or sinful. Such writing has no "redeeming social value." You usually do it quietly, and become a closet-writer. Journal-keeping while in therapy (or trauma), academic writing, prayer diaries, business memos, and sailor's logs — all are quasi-respectable forms of writing. But writing merely as a pastime or hobby has a negative connotation: it seems self-centered, and, to many people, a waste of time.

Even if you do really want to write for a larger audience, or think you *should* because someone praised your lively letters or creative holiday greeting, the myths about "real" writers (meaning professional or serious writers) may detract from your enjoyment of writing and continue to limit your possibilities.

My own litany of illusions about "real writers," usually meaning everybody except me, went as follows: "Real writers have talent, intelligence, degrees. Real writers are exciting, inspired, creative. Real writers love to write and write easily (or at least more easily than I do). Real writers are free spirits, amoral, and live adventurous lives. Real writers are rich, have secretaries, travel to exotic places. Real writers get published early, effortlessly, and often.

In the midst of this confusing and discouraging head trip, I also kept searching for the definition of a writer that felt right for me, one that felt achievable.

The definition I kept posted over my desk for a couple of years said: "A writer is someone who wrote this morning!" It's helpful to post a simple reminder of the daily commitment to the writing life, whether your aim is to write professionally or to pursue pleasurable self-expression.

I also like what Jessamyn West says about being a writer: "To be a writer, you have to first stick your neck out and take a chance and then be willing to make a fool of yourself and give yourself away." That kind of a risk was not a part of my early ideas about being a writer, but that *is* the reality.

Eric Hoffer, a self-educated longshoreman, said:

> *They who lack talent expect things to happen with-*
> *out effort. They ascribe failure to a lack of education or*
> *inspiration or ability, or to misfortunes, rather than to*
> *insufficient application.*
>
> *At the core of every true talent there is an awareness*
> *of the difficulties inherent in any achievement, and the*
> *confidence that by persistence and patience, something*
> *worthwhile will be realized. Thus talent is a species of*
> *vigor.*[1]

The French novelist Balzac commented about the life-style of the writer: "We must have order in our lives so we can go crazy in our work." Again, not what I thought.

Another reality many are unprepared for, if writing for publication is really the desire, is the necessity for serving an apprenticeship.

Among my more persistent illusions about writing is the belief that it becomes easier the longer I keep at it. While it is true that things do get easier, standards and goals escalate too, so there's always a sense of stretching (or of impossibility).

In spite of knowing all this, the "if onlys" continue to rear their ugly heads. "If only I had more time, money, encouragement; if only I had fewer demands from family and job; then I could write more, write better, and be more successful." There's a grain of truth in some of these complaints, but I've learned that when I have something I passionately want to say, I get it done no matter what. People *do* make room in their lives for what is important to them.

Prospective students often tell me: "I'm going to write when the kids are in school, or when they leave home, or when I retire." My usual reply is: "If you're not doing it now — in some small way — it probably isn't important enough." And it may never happen unless you start *now*.

WORDPLAY #5

Dump out onto paper all your beliefs about writing, writers, and yourself as a writer. Add your own "if only" list. *Write without thinking, without stopping.* Take only five to ten minutes. Afterwards, go back and read over what you've listed. Circle those beliefs which are useful and draw a line through any limiting beliefs or "if onlys."

Much of my inspiration comes from other crafts. For instance, R.D. Culler talks about boatbuilding:

> *Do it. That's what it's all about: any man who wants can produce a good boat. It takes some study, some practice, and, of course, experience.*
>
> *The experience starts coming the minute you begin and not one jot before. I sometimes hear the wail, 'I have no experience.'*
>
> *Start. Start anything and experience comes.*
>
> *As one of my friends says, 'It's only a boat; go ahead and build it.' If the first effort is a bit lumpy, so what? There will be another less lumpy later on.*[2]

So, the creation of "lumpy" writings can be a useful form of apprenticeship.

7

Escape Writing Versus Escape Reading

Everybody knows what escape reading is. It's any kind of reading done for diversion or pleasure, to temporarily escape from the daily grind and relax the mind. Fiction is a favorite form of escape reading; it allows us to vicariously enjoy lives of suspense, drama, romance, or fantasy.

Biography and autobiography offer us other escape reading, as in the books about (or by) Jackie Kennedy, Jane Fonda, Michael Jackson, O. J. Simpson, and other celebrities. Armchair travelers can enjoy the *Conquest of Everest* or *Blue Highways*. Cookbooks of any size, shape, or form are perennial bestsellers, possibly because, as one survey has shown, more people read cookbooks for pleasure or escape, than as serious cooking guides. A new area of escape reading covers the diet, exercise, and healthy-lifestyle books. Self-help and how-to books fall into this category as well. I suspect they are more often read for diversion than with serious intent.

We may rationalize our willingness to change or do what is suggested, but our action is the proof. A few people will take action as a result of this kind of reading. The rest, like it or not, are pure escape readers. They escape into the illusion of "I'll diet (or exercise or build that birdhouse or write that poem) tomorrow."

I confess to being a compulsive reader, a compulsive book buyer (especially self-help books), and a compulsive book pusher. That's why I know so much about escape reading. For me, reading is sometimes a vice rather than a virtue, because it has often absorbed the time I had to do my own writing. Ultimately it comes down to the question: "Do I want to be a writer or a reader? Active or passive?"

What I'd like to propose here is that you consider becoming an escape writer instead of an escape reader. That you write for pleasure, the pleasure of creating your own world, your own adventures, your own dramas and dreams. You can write the kind of thing you normally read as diversion or for escape. You can even make up the stories and entertainments you'd like to read. "Just for the fun of it!"

WORDPLAY #6

Make a list of the reading you do, taking five to fifteen minutes. Who are your favorite authors? What forms of writing do you prefer? (Books? Magazines? Poems? Novels? Fantastic universes? Romantic adventures? Letters to the editor?) How much time each week do you spend on this kind of reading, or in similar pursuits such as watching television? What sorts of things would you like to write? The emphasis in this approach is on fun — not technique, not literature, not with an eye on publication. This is a just-for-fun enjoyment, to entertain oneself.

The truth is that many of today's best-read authors started out writing just for themselves or a group of friends. Jane Austen wrote *Pride and Prejudice* for her family. Anais Nin's *Diaries* originally were written for herself and the father from whom she was separated. They were not intended for publication. Her serious work, surreal fiction, never caught on and she ultimately realized that the *Diaries* were her important work. Louisa May Alcott put pen to paper to exorcise a horrendous childhood. Emily Dickinson, the poet, wrote for herself and her salvation, to escape from a circumscribed existence. She was published only after her death.

Flaubert, the 19th century French novelist, said in a letter to a friend:

> *To be well known is not my main business; it can only be entirely satisfying to those with a poor conceit of themselves. Besides, even then does one ever know when to rest content? The utmost reknown never slakes a man's appetite and, unless he is a fool, he almost always dies uncertain of his own fame....if your work of art is good, if it is right, it will evoke its response, it will find its place, in six months' time, in six years, or when you are dead. What does it matter?*[1]

Some writers I've known who have started out believing they wanted to (or should) write for publication have ended up unpublished, but not unsuccessful, since they did not stop writing. They found out that the act of writing, the process of writing, was so satisfying for them that they couldn't quit. It was the personal value they derived from their writing, *not* seeing it in print, that was most important.

Humorist Peg Bracken said, "Everyone should write their own memoir to leave a personal record," and I would add, "to increase the value and pleasure from that life."

Writing can also be a form of healing. Many of my students, as they write about their encounters with illness or death, have reached a level of acceptance and understanding that has surprised them. One student began writing because of an arthritic condition in her hands that led her doctor to advise her to take up typing or knitting. Creating her own worlds of science fiction on the typewriter appealed to her more than endlessly knitting sweaters.

It took a long time for me to recognize and acknowledge how much value I've derived from the copious writing I've done since that first writing class. Much of it is unpublished; it has not even been rejected, since it never got that far. My collection includes over 50 spiral notebooks ranging from 70 to 200 pages each, full of the bits and pieces of my life: story and article ideas; observations, perceptions, amusing conversations; mundane lists of what-I'm-going-to-do-today, followed by grumblings because I didn't get it all done. It's all pretty haphazard, but wonderfully rich, rich in value for me.

When prowling through my collection, I experience both pleasure and embarrassment. The pleasure comes from the ideas and the variety, and the embarrassment is over how few of them were taken to completion. Nevertheless, I feel great satisfaction in having done them at all; a satisfaction divorced from good/bad, right/wrong, and publishable/unpublishable considerations.

Anybody can derive value from writing: not just journal writing, but writing novels and stories and entertainments just for the fun of it.

I neither advocate nor believe that anybody can (or should) write for publication. I do believe that nurturing an idea, and playing around with it — giving it life on paper — is both worthwhile and potentially satisfying. The satisfaction of creating worlds and visions and dreams that come alive is within the reach of anybody who has the desire!

Many closet-writers need to look at their writing in this light. Many would-be writers need to challenge their intent. They need to admit, at least to themselves, that they really want to write for the fun of it. They also need to admit that their own pleasure or satisfaction, or that of a small circle of friends or relatives, is justification enough, and acknowledge that the act of writing as an outlet for creativity/self-expression is a fine and noble pursuit.

In my writing each day I seek a sense of accomplishment in my involvement with the process of putting words on paper. Pleasure and fulfillment, pure and simple, are what I hope to gain by writing, and sometimes what I experience!

Doctor and author George Sheehan wrote:

> *If you are doing something you would do for nothing — then you are on your way to salvation. And if you could drop it in a minute and forget the outcome, you are even further along. And if while you are doing it you are transported into another existence, there is no need for you to worry about the future.*[2]

8

The Reality of Writing

An idea sparks. Excitement flares and ignites. I want to write it down. To play around with it just to see what might happen. To see what connections will occur in the exploration. To exult and revel (and sometimes wallow) in the magnificent richness of the English language. To go to excess. To indulge myself in looking for analogies and examples to show what I mean. I want to capture that idea before it gets away.

I find paper and pen and sit down to begin. If I'm lucky, one sentence may straggle onto paper before a lot of other things start happening, things that sometimes interfere with the flow of my writing.

It used to be that the critical/evaluative side of me would control the writing process. That watchdog crouching on my left shoulder who knows about "good" and "bad" writing would look at the first sprawling sentence or two and read it over. It then whispered (or shouted) in my ear: "What kind of a first sentence is that? It doesn't even have a verb."

The other part of me, the part that gets excited by ideas, excited by words, excited about writing, is about five years old. It's curious, friendly, and excitable, with an I-can't-wait-to-tell-you-about-it kind of enthusiasm, a jumping-up-and-down kind of youthful impatience. However, being five years old, it's also interested in being approved of and liked.

So, when it got stopped by the watchdog's criticism, it scratched out the offending sentence and tried again. Tried to please. Tried to get it right. Tried very hard to get something with a verb in it, even though it's not quite sure what a verb is. The childlike part of me worked at trying to be careful.

Finally, the five-year-old would get another first sentence and look to the watchdog for approval. The watchdog would look at the new sentence, sigh deeply, and say something like, "Well, I suppose, if that's the best you can do...." And then, the no-longer-excited child got to eke out each sentence under close supervision.

And that's not any fun. The excitement, the spontaneity, and eagerness to share was gone. No wonder I didn't really like to write for a couple of years. No wonder so many would-be writers are intimidated by the idea of writing. No wonder people get discouraged. No wonder writing is something so many think they just can't do.

We can often blame this stifling of our creativity on much of our traditional education. From the time we start school (or sometimes even before), when we are first given paper and pencil or crayon, we are admonished: "Think before you write," "Be neat," "Do it right."

We are taught to engage the rational, thinking, logical part of ourselves the minute we pick up a pen and face a piece of blank paper. Gradually, this response becomes automatic. Paper plus pen equals "think first."

If we don't get totally discouraged by this sterile, no-fun approach to writing, we learn to be logical and safe and correct in our writing at all costs. And it's usually dull and boring, and often not truthful. Telling the truth is not experienced as a safe thing to do. We learn to write to meet someone else's expectations rather than to explore our own excitements and experiences, our own truths in our writing.

It's as if the excitable five-year-old gets to write only with a punitive, watchful adult sitting firmly on its lap, or at least looking sternly over its shoulder, to make sure it is done right. To make sure there is no goofing off.

The first stage or first draft of any writing needs to be a creative stage, a time to play and explore ideas, "to fingerpaint with words." Writing safely and carefully too soon limits our possibilities.

It's useful to get a sense of the split between the part of you that wants to do it right — the part that has gone to school and has had parents, the grownup part — and the playful child part that wants to share excitement and ideas, and likes the feel of playing with words on paper.

My suggestion is that when you want to write something, take your grownup/watchdog firmly by the scruff of its neck and lock it in the closet. Do not throw away the key. Your watchdog/critic will be very useful later on in the second stage of writing, the rewriting stage.

Now that the watchdog is safely out of the way, the excited child, the creative part of you, wants to write. It scribbles a first sentence onto the paper. Nobody is looking. Nobody is making impossible demands. So, it gets to keep playing around with the words on paper, the bits and pieces, the possibilities of the idea — all the interesting connections and sidetracks.

"A creative mind is rarely tidy," declares a poster hanging in my office. This first-stage process of wordplay is often very messy, very chaotic, rarely tidy. It lacks precision in language. It tends toward primitive expression. It indulges in puns and colorful metaphors. It doesn't know or care about paragraphs, punctuation, or logical progression of thought. Expressing creativity, aliveness, truth, is what it's all about. That's what it's really doing.

This can't-sit-still youthful creator, once it gets started with nobody to inhibit it, can get happily absorbed in writing, sometimes for hours at a stretch. It loses track of time. It experiences pleasure.

After a while, it runs out of steam, leaving a mess of paper with words all over it. At that point, it can unlock the closet and call the watchdog/critic in for a consultation.

"Look," it says, "What do you think? What do I do now?"

The watchdog/critic, who is very good at thinking, looks at the first sentence and says: "What kind of a first sentence is that? It doesn't even have a verb." *The same comment as before!* But now it has a chance to play a useful role.

It looks down the first page or two and, somewhere in those first few paragraphs or pages, it finds something that meets its standards. It says, "Here's where this piece really begins. Let's take this part and put it there," and "I get the idea of what you want here, but an example might be better."

Then, it can give concrete directions for rewriting, for taking the ideas or sections and rearranging them in a logical and persuasive order. So the writing/rewriting process becomes a collaboration between the creative mind (first-stage writing) and the critical one (second-stage rewriting). And it's totally harmonious, and useful. The finished piece has the excitement of the child and the orderliness of the grownup.

If your first draft doesn't come alive, doesn't crackle with excitement, it's unlikely that a second draft will. What you want to capture in your first writing is that aliveness, that excitement, that crackle!

9

Getting Hooked
on Writing

I t's a Sunday morning and a writing day for me. I'm wearing navy sweat pants, a turquoise jacket, purple socks (my lucky purple socks), and pink jogging shoes. I just returned from forty minutes of roving (a combination of brisk walking and easy jogging). I'm no athlete, but I get out in the fresh air each day to stimulate the creative flow. The rhythmic movements and deeper breathing pull oxygen into my brain, loosen up my body, and dust away the mental cobwebs.

As I jogged past two churches, I saw people all dressed up, coming from or going to religious services, and it occurred to me that my writing days, my writing time, had become sacred for me. My ritual includes roving in the fresh air, a giant cup of coffee, a quiet working space, and the preliminary five-minute dumping of daily irritations and worries into my journal, all of which help to bring me as fresh and as empty as possible to my desk.

At my desk, I take dictation from my playful five-year-old self, making myself available to tap into a kind of collective creativity. And I religiously set aside and protect my time for writing, showing up each writing day to see what will happen.

At my desk I wrestle with the demons of self-doubt. I perform an act of faith that a certain book, or story, or train of thought might, in the long run, turn out to have been worth doing, to have been worth telling, to have been worth the time, the energy, and the hard labor.

I study creative principles, my own creative process, to learn enough about myself to discover what works and what doesn't work for me. I continue to learn from the time-honored trial-and-error-and-error-and-error method.

I keep showing up, to work through my fears. Woody Allen, humorist and filmmaker, said: "Ninety per cent of life is showing up." Fred Gwynne, actor and writer, said: "Ninety per cent of talent is lack of fear."

My daily roving in the nearby park functions not only to stimulate the creative flow, but also provides a perfect analogy for my writing process. If I've not run for a while, my body feels draggy as I begin the course. It's difficult to keep going for a whole minute at a slow jog, even downhill to the beach. My muscles tire quickly. Aches and pains surface. "I just can't do it," I think.

I encourage myself to keep going anyway. The first ten to fifteen minutes alongside the water are the hardest. Sometimes, I slow to a walk or pause to catch my breath. But I press on. "Keep going," I tell myself over and over.

Then comes "Heartbreak Hill," a steep trail switchbacking up to the top of the bluff. I aim to climb it steadily with as few stops as possible. When I do pause, gasping loudly and sweating, I wonder if it's worth it. But I'm at the point of no return. It's as far to go back the way I came as to press on. So onward and upward I go. The view from the top helps me regain my breath. Then comes my second wind. I start to run, feeling limbered up. There's a sense of ease and strength and purpose. And pleasure.

I just keep on — keep on — keep on. It feels effortless, until the path rises again. If I keep my eyes down, looking for that next step, and take each one as it comes, I tend to notice the grade much less. If I fix my gaze at the top, seeing how steep it looks, I tire more quickly.

Sometimes I slow down and walk for a while. Finally I'm at the top. Then comes the best part, a slight downgrade all the way home. It's like flying. No stress. No strain. Just the pure joy of movement, of physical expression. I don't ever want to stop.

The end of my course is in sight. I've persevered, had a workout, and experienced pleasure as well as discouragement. And I've made it!

Each day thereafter, even if I only run three or four days a week, it usually gets easier. Except for the odd day. On that day, I don't even feel like getting up or getting dressed, never mind going outside to run. I feel like I'm coming down with a cold, or something worse, but I really don't want to lose momentum, so I walk out the door and begin to move.

My body is leaden. I've forgotten how to breathe. My legs work funny. My side hurts, my head aches, each step is hard labor. Following the trail to the bluff is agony. It never gets much easier, just a few minutes when it's less worse. And finally, relief that it's over. I survived. "Never again," I think.

But the next morning, I usually can't wait to get started, and the ease and pleasure are heightened. The important thing is that each day brings a different experience. Doing it anyway, especially on the hard days, is always worth it. Once in a while, I get a string of bad days in a row. The challenge is to keep on, knowing it will get easier.

Writing is exactly like that for me. Always, when starting a new project, it takes a while to get into condition, to get the hang of it, to gain momentum. Some days, you just go through the motions, maintaining the schedule, doing it today, doing it anyway.

I need to keep to a regular schedule at my desk, and I need to protect and guard that time against the encroachment of phone calls, domestic tasks, distractions, or interruptions. Sometimes, when an emergency occurs, I just give myself time-out, with no extra penalty. The extra time it takes to get back into the flow is penalty enough.

What I'm aiming for with my writing, as well as my running, is making a habit of it. It's been said that it takes twenty-one days to make or break a habit, to retrain our automatic responses, to condition ourselves in an unfamiliar way. If I can get past that twenty-first day in my writing, or my running, I've established a familiar routine, and I feel deprived if I have to miss out on the experience.

In running, there's a physiological reason for this. The running stimulates the production of endorphins in the brain, and these endorphins, natural, morphine-like substances, stimulate feelings of pleasure and well-being. Thus I've become addicted to repeating the experience or I will suffer withdrawal symptoms. I am, in short, hooked! But I'm hooked on a "positive addiction," one which reinforces itself and has a beneficial influence on the addict's quality of life.

Getting hooked on writing, the habit of writing, is my desire and challenge. With writing, there's no physiological addiction. Writing is a sedentary business, the application of the seat of the pants to the seat of the chair, the words to the page. It is also physically, mentally, and emotionally demanding.

Nevertheless, the habit of writing can become a positive addiction, so that a missed day at my desk evokes withdrawal symptoms. I think this works for me because the regular practice of writing provides stimulation to the right hemisphere of the brain. That creative right brain is the source both of emotional feelings and the experience of pleasure.

Ideas sparking, plus words flowing, plus pages accumulating equals pleasure. I get hooked on that daily source of pleasure.

A former student, who'd been blocked from writing for a long time, dropped me a note.

"I'm writing again," he said. "It's better than sex."

WORDPLAY #7

Here's a five-to-seven minute warmup that will help flex those writing muscles. Take a word or an idea and play with it. Any word. Any idea. Whatever strikes your fancy at the moment.

For example, here's one of mine:

Ideas — exciting, delightful. I like the sensuous feel of sprawling words on paper — gloriously messy. Satisfying, like fingerpainting. The smoothness of notebook paper, of different pens gliding along its surface. I like struggling with an idea, clothing it in words or coordinating its wardrobe, and sending it out fetchingly dressed to catch the attention of the world. I like that part of the process where it's like a big jigsaw puzzle, rearranging and re-ordering the ideas to make a logical picture with the fragments. I like to share ideas, communicate with an unseen audience. It's scary and marvelous when the creative flow begins and floods. The challenge: to hang in there when I'm stuck or blocked until something happens, until something moves. Practicing what I preach about writing is humbling, sometimes humiliating, but often fulfilling. I'm happy when I'm learning. Words on paper always means learning. Word-tripping is fun, pure and simple.

10

The Power of "You"niqueness

M ost of us tend to devalue or downgrade our personal experience of life and learning. It's as if the everyday, ordinary events, and even the special ones, aren't special enough to be talked about, much less written about.

And yet, that's all we have to offer, to share with others. Ourselves. Our opinions. Our experiences. Our uniqueness ("you"niqueness).

I used to envy anyone who had a normal childhood or happy school experiences. Mine were hidden in a box labeled "Miserable Childhood." I didn't think anyone would be interested, even after I started writing.

One day in a workshop, a woman complained about the regimentation of her childhood, her lack of personal freedom in growing up. I envied her the family closeness that had been part of it. So I told her about my lack of supervision and about my feeling that no one had cared. I mentioned my peculiar on-again, off-again education and my tomboyhood, spent hiding out in trees with a stack of books.

The whole class not only listened, but also reflected fascination — and envy.

"Tell us more," they said.

"You should write a book about it," someone added.

Up to that point, it simply hadn't occurred to me that my growing-up experiences might be useful writing material. I began thinking about my experiences in a different way. I realized that I could lift out the bits and pieces, the anecdotes, conversations, and mini-dramas. I could sort through them, putting some of them in a box newly labeled "Unconventional Childhood."

My mother had a button box, full of buttons in all colors, sizes, and shapes. I hated sewing. (My dolls were naked and neglected more often than not.) But the button box, a round blue metal tin with a gold scroll design on top, intrigued me.

I always needed buttons for projects that consisted of paper, wood, or yarn. (For those projects that required gumption.) I'd paw through the box, then dump it out on the rug, touching all the various textures, looking for the buttons that matched or, at least, were the right size.

My fascination with the button box often sidetracked my projects. I'd sort the buttons by size, by color, by shape. Seldom were any two alike. Some, however, could be grouped together even though they weren't identical.

My experiences are like that button box: they are a place to find just the right touch to finish off a story or project. Look at how many of them popped up to be used in this book!

Nowadays, I play with other boxes full of my rich and varied experiences. From my box labeled "Child-bearing and Heir-raising" comes "The PTA Dress" (about the only item in my wardrobe that made me feel grownup enough to be a parent). From my "Naive Divorcee" box comes "Freelance Human Being" (my answer to "what do *you* do?"

in my search for an identity past motherhood and marriage), and "My Hitchhiker" (about a trip to California and my unexpected encounter with someone who felt like an old friend from the first moment we met).

All useful. All valuable. All potentially interesting to other people. My experiences are relevant both to people with similar experiences — similar in the human feeling sense — and to those with different or opposite experiences, because they satisfy a curiosity about how the other half lives.

Unfortunately, while growing up, we are admonished not to brag, not to put ourselves forward. We are supposed to be modest — false modesty I call it. We are told to reform our bad habits, to behave better, and improve. It's made very clear to us that we are not okay the way we are.

All these influences lead us to invalidate our own experience, and sometimes we hesitate before making decisions. We often look to authorities for answers, for guidelines, for permission. We check things out — first with teachers and parents, then with the government or therapists, or other so-called experts.

Sometimes the first step towards unlocking the writer within each of us is to reclaim the power and authenticity of our own experience. *If you're old enough to read this to yourself, you have all the experience you need to begin to write. If you're over forty, you have all the experience you'll ever need to write and write and write and never run out of interesting things to write about.*

I can just hear the protests at this point. "But I had an ordinary (or happy) childhood." "But I'm just a postal clerk (or mother or janitor)." "I've never traveled." "I've never sinned or suffered enough to have anything to write about."

"Horsefeathers!" I say. What do you like or dislike? Who do you love or hate? What frightens or fascinates you? Where were you when President Kennedy (or Reagan) was shot? What did you do, say, and feel? What was your experience of falling in love (or like, or lust) for the first time? What has thrilled or disappointed you? Who has had a more interesting life than you? How do you feel about that? What are your dreams? Your daydreams? Your fantasies?

All these things are your experience. All these things are worth writing about. If that doesn't seem like much, or enough, to set you to writing, in the next chapter you'll find some suggestions that may stimulate you, and get you excited.

If you've had difficulty trusting yourself, trusting the power of your own experience, perhaps you'll trust me for a while. Trust my years of helping people become writers, helping writers find their voice and write their books, helping people get from where they are with their writing, or dreams of writing, to where they want to go.

"Trust me," I ask new students. "There's method in my madness."

I assure you that *anybody can write*. What's true is that a lot of people don't even want to. But if you want to, you can do it. All you need is the willingness to experience doing it. Anybody can write — *if they want to.*

11

The Writing Experience

U p to this point, you've had the opportunity to do a little *Wordplay,* but mostly you've been reading about writing. You've read about the possibility of *you* writing, about the value of words on paper, about doing it easily, or at least doing it. We've talked about having fun with it, about giving yourself permission to do it just for your own enjoyment, and about expressing your ideas, your creativity, your uniqueness.

Now, it's time to experience it. The first writing process I'll describe is a model which embodies some useful and versatile techniques for changing your experience of writing. This three-part writing experience is deceptively simple. You may think it sounds childish or frivolous, or peculiar, at best. It may be all those things, but I guarantee that if you'll try it, especially try to get into the spirit of it, you'll find it surprisingly valuable.

What you're going to be asked to do with words on paper may feel somewhat strange, unless you had a very creative third- or fourth-grade teacher. Think of this process as another warmup, a five-finger exercise, a zero draft. A zero draft is one that doesn't count. It can be wadded up and thrown away if you don't like it. A zero draft is sometimes done on the back of used paper, so there's no waste if it doesn't work out. The main things to remember are: *write without thinking, and write without stopping.*

How can you write without thinking? You just keep putting words on paper without demanding that they make sense. As a world champion thinker, I can sit and think, or pace and think, for four hours straight. I will think about what I want to write, what I should write, where to begin. Think. Think. Think. And I get nothing on the page. *Thinking is not writing.* Writing is words on paper.

So, if thoughts come up like "This is a foolish thing for a grown person to be doing," or "I don't think I really know how to do this, I don't know what is expected of me," or "I wish I were out sailing instead," write them down as they pop up for you. Write them down right in the middle of a sentence if you need to.

What I discovered about this freeflow writing process is that there's no right way to do it. There's no wrong way to do it either. There's just doing it or not doing it.

The other rule to remember, besides the not-thinking, is: *keep the pen moving across the paper steadily the whole time.* No pausing to figure out the right word. Leave a space if you need to and continue on. No stopping to wonder what to do next. No stopping the flow of words onto paper. If you're using a typewriter or word processor the same principle applies. Keep going until the time is up. (It helps to set a timer when you first try this.)

This don't-think/don't-stop approach seems to enable us to bypass the critic, stimulate our creative flow, and have fun with our writing. The secret is to feel free enough to just put anything down on paper, especially if you feel stuck or blocked. Simply write down what's true for you about the writing process. "I feel stuck. I don't know where to go from here. I don't have anything more to say about this. I wish the time was up."

Generally, what will happen (if you're willing to acknowledge the obvious) is that you will get bored before you can cover half a page with "I-feel-stucks." Then, you'll get back on track and find yourself doing what you want to do or what you've been asked to do.

WRITING EXERCISE #1
PAPER AND PEN CONVERSATION

This is a three-part exercise. I suggest you take at least five minutes for each part. Or, write two or three pages for each part or until you feel stuck — then do one more page, or half a page past the point where you got stuck.

All you need is paper and pen, or typewriter, and a little gumption. *Write steadily. No thinking. No stopping. No right way. No wrong way. Just do it.*

PART 1: For the next five minutes, or three pages, you are to become the piece of paper you've chosen to write on (or the screen if you're using a word processor). Use the first person, the "I" point of view. For instance: "I am the piece of paper (or CRT) that Jean chose to write on today. I was originally a piece of junk mail advertising a waterbed sale. Now my blank side gets to be useful. I'm really glad to have a chance to express myself today. I can't wait to see what I have to say...." You, the writer, make yourself available to record what the paper might have to say about itself, or about the world, today. Include its hopes and fears.

Begin now.

PART 2: Now that you've given the paper you're using a chance to express itself, it's only fair to do the same for the writing instrument you're using, whether pen, typewriter, or computer keyboard. For instance: "I'm the ballpoint pen Jean found in the bottom of her purse. I've been hiding down there for a long time. It feels good to be moving again and I feel like I have a lot to say...." Write again, for five minutes or three pages. *Have fun with it. Don't forget to write steadily.*

PART 3: Now that you've gotten these two inanimate objects talking on paper, set up a conversation between them. For example: Paper: "We're supposed to talk to each other, but I don't know how to begin." Pen: "Looks like you already have. You sure didn't give me a chance to say something first." Paper: "I can't help it if you're slower than I am." Begin now. Keep your pen moving the whole time. No stopping. No thinking. Five minutes or two to three pages. Keep going.

Postscript: Here is a last little bit that's fun to do with this process as a way of winding it up. Now that you've gotten these inanimate objects talking, it's an opportunity to find out what they might have to say to you, the writer. Write out a question to ask them. Then see what happens. For example: "What advice do you have for me today?" Paper: "I don't know about advice, but I liked having my say and hope I can do it again sometime." Pen: "Don't forget me. This couldn't have taken place without my help."

This is an easy technique for getting words on paper that you can use at any time. It's especially useful if you're just beginning to acquire the habit of writing. Just doing this for fifteen to twenty minutes each day can limber up your writing muscles, and get you comfortable with the act of putting words on paper on a regular basis.

This technique is called projection. You project your own thoughts and feelings onto whatever you're writing about. It's something we all do a lot of anyway (without necessarily being aware of it). When you're starting to practice the projection technique, pick inanimate objects, since they do not have thoughts or feelings that we can readily interpret. This is an extremely versatile process, and its usefulness to you will be limited only by your imagination. I encourage you to play with it.

WRITING EXERCISE #2
PROJECTION TECHNIQUE

Pick any object in the room, or in view, or in your mind's eye. You could pick your car, the teddy bear you had as a child, or your left tennis shoe. Make yourself available to let the object express itself on paper, using the first-person point of view, "I am...." After the object has told you as much as possible about itself, then you can talk to it. Have fun with it. Ask it questions. Record its answers. Enlist its help with the ideas you'd like to be able to write about.

Aim to do two to three pages, or spend five minutes, or write until you feel stuck and then *do one more page*. Even if that extra page is nothing but gibberish, in the long run, the willingness to *write one more page* when you feel like giving up, or think you've run out of things to say, will pay you handsome dividends.

12

"Anything Goes" Journal Magic

"Keep a journal," my first writing teacher advised. "That's the best way to get more comfortable with putting words on paper." It was obviously the way to gain more facility with the act of writing.

It was great advice. The best advice about writing I've ever gotten, as a matter of fact. But it fell on deaf ears. I really couldn't see the point of it. I could see no value in beginning what seemed like just another mindless writing chore. After all, what could you do with a journal after it was done? My notion of a journal was a place where you wrote about your feelings, an adolescent confessional, a "Dear Diary." Who needed that?

Not me! The other kind of journal I knew about intrigued me more — a writer's journal or sketchbook. A place to record story ideas, fragments of overheard dialogue, descriptions of places or seasons of the year. However, I resisted doing even that kind of a journal for almost a year.

Summer vacation approached and the prospect of no classes for three months set me looking for a writing project to do so I wouldn't lose the momentum I had gained during the school year.

Okay, I'd try a journal, but it had to be a writer's journal. I assigned myself one page a day, one side of the page, in a wide-lined notebook. And I'd do it before going to sleep at night. Lyrical descriptions, article and story ideas, scraps of conversation. Maybe even poetry!

Grand ideas! Good plan. The first day came. Night fell. I took out the notebook, rounded up a pen. I thought and thought. Scribbled a few lines, feeling dumb. I tried writing a description. It was lifeless, boring. I eked out the rest of the page, feeling frustrated.

The final line on that first page read: "You even show off your big vocabulary to yourself!" Not an auspicious beginning, with my critic taking a potshot at me.

However, I kept my agreement to do one page a day over the summer, despite the daily barbs from the critic. It was the hardest thing I'd ever done, and resulted in a somewhat boring diary rather than the exciting writer's journal I'd envisioned. But I did keep writing, hoping it would be useful.

By the time class resumed, the journal (diary) was a habit, one I've kept ever since. And it has turned out to be personally valuable, as well as serving as a source book for some of my other writings.

A journal is one of the best ways to explore writing. If you can keep the critic away, if you can allow yourself to record the truths of your life, if you can withhold judgment, the time spent on a journal can pay off more than anything else I know.

It's important to keep your journal private. It's vital that you protect it from prying eyes, or even from casual reading. Avoid showing it to friends and loved ones. Any kind of exposure to others can be detrimental.

Find the type of notebook that feels comfortable for you.

Friends often give me those fancy bound journals with heavy, unlined paper. I can't use them. I feel inhibited, as if I should improve my handwriting first, or write poetry. I require total permissiveness from my involvement with my journal!

"I've been writing in a notebook for over three years," one of my students told me. "But 'journal' is too formal a word for what I do, and diary is too juvenile. So I call it my Anything Goes Book."

'Anything Goes'! What a wonderful idea. It poses no limits on my imagination, no curbs on my creativity. And it covers all the uses to which I put my notebook — pasting in fortunes from fortune cookies, daily horoscope predictions (the good ones), love letters (outgoing and incoming) — unlimited possibilities!

Magic results from regular and longterm involvement with oneself on paper. The 'Anything Goes' type of journal is the easiest way to create this involvement. Journals need not be grim and boring. Expressing the joys of your life, exploring what's good in your life today, playing with ideas — all are potentially magical.

Lighten up! Use your journal as a portable friend and confidante. Find a good name for it such as "Horace" or "Matilda" or "Hilary," so you can tell others about some of your journal insights. "As I was telling Matilda the other day...."

The 'Anything Goes' journal could be one way to explore all the ideas in this book and invent some playful ones of your own as well. As a matter of fact, many of these processes are adaptations of journal techniques that I have discovered are useful for facilitating any kind of writing.

If you began an 'Anything Goes' notebook and did nothing but variations of the *Wordplay* suggestions for a year, I guarantee you'd be astonished and delighted with the results.

A nonthreatening, no-demands notebook which is protected and private can provide the perfect place to "write at risk," to say all the unsayable things, to tell things like they really are (like they really are for *you!*). A secret place to risk being honest with yourself.

A journal is a place to explore all the little happinesses and large joys of your unique life.

A place to have fun!

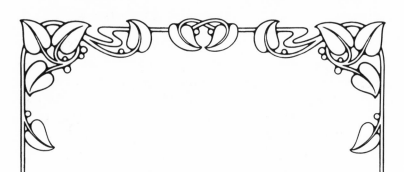

TRUSTING YOURSELF

Trust yourself. Trust your experience. Trust your feelings.

Trust your uniqueness as a vulnerable human being who has experienced life in a different way from any other individual, past or present. There are no new ideas — only new perceptions, new ways of seeing things, fresh points of view. Trust yours.

As a writer, the only thing you have to offer the world is your own unique self. Be courageous. When you think, "Oh, I can't write that part, I can't put it down; it's too petty, too shameful. It's not respectful. People won't understand." — ignore these unuseful thoughts. Say it truthfully (full truth). Trust yourself, and trust your potential reader. Trust the truth; be willing to write "at risk."

Trust your intuition, your absurdities, your loves, your hates. Most of all, trust your passions, *those extra strong feelings and urges that flow and surge and pulse with aliveness. Passion provides momentum, involvement, commitment, action. Trust it.*

PART THREE

EVERYBODY HAS DIFFICULTIES

13

Arm-wrestling Self-doubt

"Every day when I begin to write, I face that big hairy beast," one student remarked. The big hairy beast she referred to is her insecurity, her doubts about herself, the voices in her head that question, "What makes you think you have anything to say?" or "What's the use, it's all been written before," or "You can't do it well enough, so why try?"

Self-doubt assails the best of us from time to time. Even English novelist Anthony Trollope admitted, "There are some hours of agonizing doubt, almost of despair...."

Thinking too much, instead of plunging in and playing with words and ideas on paper, limits your playful energy, limits your production of pages, and limits your possibilities. Pay no attention to the gremlins of discouragement, lest you talk yourself out of writing at all, lest you lose your belief in yourself.

Be willing to experiment. As Carl Jung once wrote:

Every one of us gladly turns away from his problems; if possible, they must not be mentioned, or better still, their existence is denied. We wish to make our lives

73

simple, certain and smooth — and for that reason problems are taboo. We choose to have certainties and no doubts — results and no experiments — without even seeing that certainties can arise only through doubt, and results through experiment.

When we must deal with problems — we instinctively refuse to try the way that leads through darkness and obscurity. We wish to hear only of unequivocal results and completely forget that these results can only be brought about when we have ventured into and emerged again from the darkness. But to penetrate the darkness we must summon all the powers of enlightened thought consciousness can offer. We must even indulge in speculations.[1]

One secret of success in writing is to do that speculation *on paper*, not in your head. Overthinking results in paralysis-by-analysis. You wonder which idea to pursue or which style or point of view to use. You can't decide, so you do nothing.

Here are a couple of frivolous-sounding yet very practical ways to simplify those kinds of choices. Most people are familiar with this first one. It's called "Eeny, meeny, miney, moe." It works because if you really don't know which is best, it doesn't really make any difference. Choose any one. The second decision-making process is useful when you have only two choices. You simply flip a coin. Heads, one way. Tails, the other. The secret is to watch your emotional response to what comes up. Then follow that response, rather than the coin. Freud himself suggested this idea, the point being that the toss and your reaction to it have given you some information not in your conscious awareness.

Creative excuses often absorb writing energy. One student complained that reading her favorite authors, instead of stimulating her own work, caused her to feel "Oh, I can never do *as well as that*." She made the mistake of comparing her zero-draft explorations and beginnings with polished and professional work and said, "I can't."

Can't simply means *won't*. When writing regularly, I avoid reading the type of things I'm writing. I look for the kind of reading that inspires and renews me, but doesn't lend itself to easy comparison.

"I could try, I guess," a young man reluctantly admitted when I challenged his constant (and creative) excuses for not writing.

"Trying is an illusion," I say in class and throw a pencil on the floor to prove it. "*Try* to pick it up," I challenge.

Picking up the pencil is doing it. Not picking up the pencil is *not* doing it. In between there are only empty gestures, half-hearted movements toward what you want, that always stop short of completion. When it comes to writing, saying "I tried" is always a cop-out. There's only doing it or not doing it.

Writing is words on paper. Picking up the pen (or sitting at the typewriter) isn't enough. You must activate the tool. Lend your hand and arm and spirit and will to keeping the tool in motion. Provide the energy to keep it going.

"Easy for you to say," the lawyers in the class begin the debate. Easy to say? Of course. Easy to do? Not necessarily. It's not easy to overcome self-sabotage. It's not easy to change a lifetime of "I can'ts," "I won'ts," or "I trieds."

The first step is to be willing to do it anyway. Just keep the pen moving across the paper until your writing time is up. That's all. It's as simple (and as difficult) as that to acquire the habit of writing and the momentum that will keep you going, to prime the wellspring of ideas, creativity, and individuality that everyone possesses.

Fear is a form of self-doubt. Fear of failure. Fear of success. Fear of not pleasing someone in your life. Fear of not doing it right, not measuring up, not doing it perfectly.

Perfectionism, a child of fear, is one of the biggest killers of creativity. Unfortunately, many of the most perceptive, creative, and sensitive people are afflicted with perfectionism. Perfectionists set unrealistic standards of production or performance for themselves. They have unrealistic expectations regarding time or energy or originality or the number of drafts needed. It has been wisely said: "The pursuit of excellence is healthy and productive. The pursuit of perfection is neurotic."

It's vital to remove this performance bond from your early writings. The idea is to eliminate the success/failure trap from zero-draft, first-stage writing and cultivate an attitude of allowing things to occur. Encourage your spontaneity and playfulness.

Encourage means "to inspire with courage, spirit, or confidence. To breathe spirit into." Courage is defined as "the quality of mind or spirit that enables one to face difficulty, danger, pain, with firmness and without fear; bravery."

So, the antidote to self-doubt is courage. "The courage to be dreadful," someone once called it. And, if the critic in you refuses to stop judging, then the courage to be dreadful might be useful.

Even more useful is the realization that the critic has two voices, two personae. One says things like "You numbskull." or "How could you be so stupid?" or "That's bad." This is the destructive voice.

The constructive critic, the one worth listening to, *always tells you something you can do.* It seldom indulges in good/bad, right/wrong judgments. It says things like "That's unclear. Why don't you try this?" or "This needs a specific example to prove your point."

Challenge your internal critic to offer suggestions for improvement, not blanket indictments. Find the courage to experiment your way through the darkness and obscurity of your ideas, your problems with writing.

Confusion, which feels like a form of self-doubt, is

simply one more stage that precedes clarity. So, when I'm feeling confused, I remind myself that beyond this muddle lies the clarity I seek. And if no way through presents itself, *I do something, even if it is wrong.*

Taking action is always useful in writing. Sometimes I will simply begin to copy over a few pages already written, hoping that this action will start the flow again.

Self-doubt cannot survive that daring leap into the unknown. I often begin my writing task by spilling out onto paper, in a five-minute dump, the self-doubts of that particular day. This acknowledges them, yet doesn't allow them to interfere with the writing at hand. Here's another way to deal with self-doubt, as shown in the following *Wordplay*.

WORDPLAY #8

Write without thinking for five to ten minutes, without pausing. Do it with a sense of playfulness. Begin like this: "I am (your name)'s self-doubt and I am persistent and powerful." Then let it tell you about itself, the form it takes, the times it occurs. Let it tell you what its intention is, what it's trying to do for you, what it's trying to protect you from. Get to know it. Befriend it. Find out what it wants and how you can meet its needs in a mutually satisfying way.

This technique can be used in any situation where self-doubt or any other form of negative thinking is an obstacle.

WORDPLAY #9

Think of a favorite author, living or not, or a writer you particularly admire. Take five to ten minutes (no thinking, no stopping) to write a letter to that person, telling him or her all the things you appreciate about their writing. Then describe whatever your problem is with writing. Ask that person for advice.

In the second part of this exercise, take another five to ten minutes to write a reply from this writer to yourself, thanking you for the compliments and then giving you concrete ways to deal with the difficulty you described.

Try this technique sometime. It may sound peculiar, but like the rest of the playful ideas in this book, it can be a powerful tool.

14

Writing is Too Serious to be Taken Seriously

A Dialogue

ME: You've got to be kidding. What do you mean writing is too serious to be taken seriously? Who are you anyway?

VOICE: I am your muse. My name is Amuse. You were daydreaming, thinking you needed a muse to inspire you, so here I am.

ME: Where did you come from?

AMUSE: From your subconscious. You wanted someone to help you keep going on this book, to help you finish it on schedule. I overheard John telling you that he'd worked happily along for a couple of months, having fun with his book, until he'd shown it to a friend who'd praised it. She said it would be "powerful," and John said he hasn't touch it since.

ME: I told him to go back to having fr'
forget about anything else.

AMUSE: So here I am to remind you

thing. You've been feeling very heavy about this project, very serious, and you've slowed down.

ME: So tell me about yourself. I'm running out of time.

AMUSE: I'm the free and creative and playful part of you. I'm unconcerned about time. I prefer joy and lightness. I'm always smiling, at least in my eyes, with a mischievous appreciation of the humor of it all, a sense of the ridiculous. Wit and Wisdom were my parents. I'm always good for a laugh, a quip, the light touch. Some think me superficial, but profundity is not depth. Besides, I could care less about others' opinions. I am self-contained, seeing both self and others with a detached and delicious humor. I have a gift for making things light and easy.

ME: So how do you propose to make my involvement with this book light and easy?

AMUSE: My message to you is "amuse thyself," which is what you're doing at this moment. What else can I do for you?

ME: I can't seem to seriously settle down to work today.

AMUSE: If you're determined to be serious, I can't help. What do you really want?

ME: I want to feel good about my writing again. I feel so shut down I can hardly breathe, but I don't know what that has to do with my book. I keep trying to stay on topic, to the point. I keep trying to honor my commitment to get this done on time.

AMUSE: Oh dear! On topic. To the point. Commitment. Time. How grim. How limiting. You say you want to feel good. What would it take?

ME: I don't know. I keep going through the motions, but I'm tending to stay stuck and safe. No joy, no fun, but no pain either. I don't like being so fearful and stuck.

AMUSE: Why not enjoy feeling stuck?

ME: How can I do that?

AMUSE: How can you not? Think (pardon the expression) about it. Let's hear it for the joys of feeling stuck!

ME: Are you making fun of me?

AMUSE: More like fun *for* you. I'm always on your side, but not always the side you'd expect! Okay, the choices are: (1) feeling stuck and denying it, (2) admitting feeling stuck, but not liking it, and (3) feeling stuck and wallowing in it, surrendering to it, even, heaven forfend, enjoying it. Your choice.

ME: I'll give wallowing a try. Stuck. Mired. Quiet. Safe. Stuck. Muffled. No energy. No smiles. No joy. No pain. Just evenness, going through the motions. No emotions, just motions. Stop moving. Be stuck. Truly stuck. Unmoving. Unmoved. Paralyzed. Immobile. Dead. Safe. Nothing. Stuck. Stuck. Horrible word!

AMUSE: Why horrible? Stuck is a funny word.

ME: Funny? Nothing's fun. Nothing's funny.

AMUSE: But you just said stuck was nothing. Then you said nothing's funny. Therefore, stuck is a funny word.

ME: You're twisting it!

AMUSE: One of my harmless diversions. Twisting words and meanings and following peculiar connections. I really enjoy doing that! Now, where were we?

ME: I was wallowing. You weren't taking me seriously.

AMUSE: That's right! Say, why don't you try a humorous essay about writer's blocks?

ME: Okay.

WRITERS'S BLOCKS MAKE GREAT WALLS

Here's a handy reference guide to seven of the most common writer's blocks. Very useful for stuck-o walls.

Block #1 — Think Before You Write: Think about what

you want to say. Think about how it better be done correctly, how it better be good and original or, at the least, properly grammatical. Think about everyone who might read it, especially your mother. Get a fresh cup of coffee and think some more.

Block #2 — Do Research Instead: It's probably important that you know everything about kiwi fruit or Parisian brothels or how to stalk, kill, eviscerate, and roast a wild boar before you tackle that next chapter. Do your research in person if possible. Travel is good for the writer. Don't even begin your writing until your research is complete.

Block #3 — Get Plenty of Advice: Show your first pages, or a partial draft, to your spouse or "significant other," to your friends, maybe even to your dentist. Ignore the fact that one definition of a camel is a horse assembled by a commmittee. Take all the advice you get. Don't trust yourself.

Block #4 — Take Everything Personally: If you are lavishly praised, or hailed as the new Hemingway or Erma Bombeck, don't bother to rewrite anything. Send it out to be published immediately and, when it's rejected, stop writing altogether. If your work is criticized, if they say it's not perfect, assume it's *you* they don't like. Pout, sulk, and complain about your unfair treatment.

Block #5 — Wait for Inspiration: Check your horoscope for the day. And your biothythms. If your lucky purple socks are in the wash, do the laundry instead. Organize your desk while you wait — at least you're near the typewriter. Clean the keys and change the ribbon. If your muse continues to play coy, go to a movie. You may want to write a screenplay someday.

Block #6 — Procrastinate! Procrastinate! Procrastination is a magnificent prioritizer. Just think, if you can postpone it long enough, you may not have to write it at all. Someone else will do it anyway. Never write today. Tomorrow will be better.

Block #7 — Always Be Serious: Never be satisfied with less than perfection. Remember how significant this needs to be. Don't forget for one moment how much is riding on the completion of this project. You could lose face, lose credibility, or lose your job if you botch it up — don't forget that. Also, don't let the heaviness of that knowledge bother you too much. The resulting writer's cramp, or paralysis of will, usually disappears in a year or two, after the danger is past.

15

Persistence and Other Useful Attitudes

A ll my life, I've had a love/hate affair with the word discipline. It's what I thought I wanted and needed to be successful as a writer, or in any other endeavor. It's definitely what other people told me I needed.

So I sought it, but never felt as if I found it. Or, if I did, I couldn't keep it for any length of time. At least two-thirds of my students initially tell me that's what they're looking for in a class. "If only I were more disciplined...," they complain.

What I've discovered about discipline is that it has a joyless quality to it. Most of us, being fallible human beings, will fall short of our desires and expectations regarding discipline anyway.

Experience, however, has taught me that there's something even better than discipline. Persistence! Persistence is achievable. Persistence is possible even when discipline is lacking. Maybe they sound the same to you, but there is a significant difference.

Looking up the definition of both words, I was struck by the negativity of the word discipline. The definition of persistence just felt more positive, more like something I really wanted.

Discipline

1. training to act in accordance with rules. Synonym: chastisement, castigation. See: punish, correction.

Persistence

1. to continue steadily, especially in spite of opposition. Synonym: persevering, steadfast, resolute. See: stubborn.

No wonder most of us have trouble with discipline. And you simply don't need discipline at all if you have stubbornness. Calvin Coolidge knew the value of persistence. He said:

Press on. Nothing in the world can take the place of persistence. Talent will not; nothing is more common than unsuccessful men with talent. Genius will not; unrewarded genius is almost a proverb. Education alone will not; the world is full of educated derelicts. Persistence and determination alone are omnipotent.[1]

Therefore, persistence is perhaps the most useful attribute. It goes beyond even faith. It's simply "doing it anyway."

Enthusiasm, passion, and Einstein's "holy curiosity" all are galvanizing, and often the impetus for any project, written or otherwise. Follow your passions, your enthusiasm, and your curiosity. If they sustain you throughout the process, you won't even need persistence.

If, however, your enthusiasm dwindles, and you feel like quitting, try doing just that. Quit! My advice to students is often, "If at first you don't succeed, quit!" When they reply, "But I can't let go of the idea," or "It won't let me be," then I say, "If you find you can't quit, can't give up the dream, or the doing, then never give up. Persevere. Keep on keeping on."

Dorothea Brande, in a self-help book first published in 1936, advised, "Act as if it were impossible to fail."[2]

Ann Gowen Combs, a former student, used a variation of this philosophy to actualize her dream of becoming a columnist. She'd been moderately successful in having her humorous personal-experience articles published, mostly in the Sunday magazine sections of the local newspapers. While in class, she worked on a book based on her family's experiences while remodeling an older home. An agent had kept the book for a year before returning it, advising her that it needed a ghost, or some sex, to be salable. She had set the book aside.

One day after class, Ann told me, "What I really want is to be a columnist." She said she'd already approached two metropolitan newspapers in person. Since they had both published her work and knew its quality, she proposed to do a column for them, similar to the humor features they'd been buying from her. She reported that the editors at both papers had been cordial but firmly discouraging, saying that they seldom used columns that weren't produced by staff. Besides, so much material was available to them through the newspaper syndicates.

Suddenly, I had a brainstorm.

"Ann, are you sure you want to be a columnist?"

"I just said I did."

"If you really want to be a columnist, I'll tell you how to do it," I promised.

"Okay. How?" she challenged.

"It's simple. If you want to be a columnist, you do what columnists do."

She raised one eyebrow.

"Columnists write columns," I explained.

"Really?" She had a hard time keeping the sarcasm out of her voice.

I continued. "If you'll write a column every week for twenty-six weeks, I guarantee that at the end of that time you'll be a columnist."

"Twenty-six weeks? Guaranteed? I'll do it," she promised.

"At the end of that time you'll have two things." I continued. "First, you'll have the week-in, week-out *experience* of being a columnist. Second, you'll have twenty-six columns with which to approach a newspaper syndicate."

She looked excited by the challenge.

"By the way," I added. "What newspaper do you want to write for?"

She reminded me that both papers had turned her down.

"Doesn't make any difference," I said. "Which paper?"

She named one. The other already had Erma Bombeck.

"Okay, I'd like you to find someone, anyone, who works for that paper. You are to send them a copy of your column every single week, for twenty-six weeks."

Skeptical, but willing, she found a friend-of-a-friend who worked for the advertising department of the newspaper. After sending him one column every week for several weeks, she called him up to ask how he liked them.

"Well, my wife liked one of them," he finally said.

The second time she called him, a few weeks later, he said, "I'm culling out the best to take over to the news side."

The advertising and editorial departments are independent of each other, but eventually the book review editor got the buck passed to him. Some of Ann's columns ended up on his desk and from there were passed to a second editor.

My only role in this was to encourage her to continue sending columns and to phone often enough without becoming a nuisance, so that they couldn't forget her.

One morning, nineteen weeks into the campaign, she called me.

"Guess what?" she said.

It wasn't unusual for her to call me, but I was astonished when she added, "The newspaper just called. They want me to be their columnist."

"Congratulations," I said. "I knew you could do it."

I had known she could do it, but I was flabbergasted because, to my knowledge, what had happened really couldn't be done. At least not that way!

I *had* been convinced that the creative principle was sound. If you want to be something, then do what that kind of a person does. Act as if it were impossible to fail, keep on keeping on, and don't take no for an answer.

Perseverance will win out!

One day a few months later, Ann received a letter from an east coast publisher saying he'd seen some of her columns and added, "Would you, by any chance, have a book?"

Of course she had the book about her family remodeling the older home, and sent it off to him *sans* ghost, *sans* sex. And although she did do some rewriting, it was published *sans* ghost, *sans* sex!

Richard Bach says, in his book *Illusions*, "You are never given a wish, without also being given the power to make that wish come true. You may have to work for it, however."[3]

Your power comes from the willingness to involve yourself persistently with whatever you wish to do or be. And to keep working toward it until it happens. *No matter what it takes.*

Part of what it takes is commitment — to oneself, to the dream of being a columnist or a writer or a poet or whatever. And commitment to an idea, to giving that idea life on paper.

Commitment is a measurable thing. It is not what I said

I was going to do, or what I planned to do, or what I'd like to happen. Commitment is what I actually *did*. Results determine commitment, not the other way around. Look at what you're doing, what you're actually accomplishing, to determine what you're committed to.

16

The Trial-and-Error-and-Error-and-Error Method

W hether you decide to write for your own satisfaction, for self-discovery, as an escape, as an outlet for your own creativity, or for publication, the learning process is seldom as straightforward as most of us have been led to believe.

For me, it felt like I wasted a lot of my writing time with things that didn't work out. I'd start on a story, lose interest, try it again later, maybe in a new form or from a different point of view. Maybe I would rewrite it several times, but it still didn't satisfy me.

I kept hoping I'd get better so that I would waste less time, improve my process, and raise my batting average of pieces sold. My fantasy was to sit down to write and have the right words pour out the end of my pen, ready to polish and type up. No false starts. No abortive ideas. No endless rewriting. But I just couldn't seem to do it the way I thought it was supposed to be done.

I'd been taught to plan my writing carefully, to do an

outline and stick to that outline. But that always bored me. Instead, I followed my ideas off in strange directions, sometimes never getting back to my original train of thought. Sometimes, derailed in exploring other possibilities, I ended up with successful pieces, but not necessarily what I'd started out to do.

I always felt guilty about working like that, until I heard of something called "The Correction Model." First, you do it. Then, you correct it. All my life I'd used that approach to learning, but had thought I was wrong. I wasn't! You learn by doing, by experiencing, then fixing it if necessary, but *always learning something in the process.*

The trial-and-error-and-error-and-error process for getting writing done does work. Nothing is wasted either, since something is always learned from each try, each error.

Also, I've discovered something very important about what shows up in print. Most books, stories, and articles in print represent maybe ten percent of the words originally written. The writing, rewriting, and editing process remove a large percentage of the original output — if you count from where it started on the back of an envelope down to the final typed draft. And it's all useful.

Consider an iceberg. The part that shows above the waterline only hints at the massive and stabilizing underwater foundation. Published material is similar. The material (sometimes as much as ninety per cent) that gets lost along the way, or edited out, somehow validates the part that shows. It may not be visible, but the knowledgeable eye can tell the difference between an ice floe and an iceberg. And the discriminating editor or reader can tell the difference between a piece of writing that was just dashed off and one which has evolved, having been stabilized and validated by all the words which were thrown away.

I used to feel very discouraged about material that was discarded, but I gradually learned to appreciate the usefulness of this natural selection process.

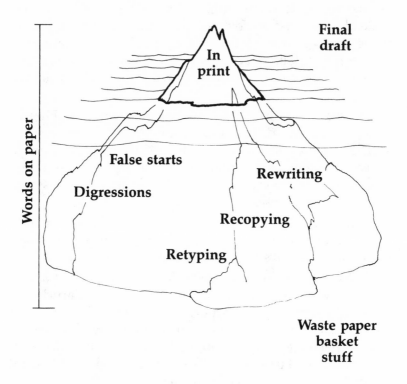

In talking to other writers and reading about successful authors, those who've been publishing for years, I learned there is a wide variety in the ratio of words written to words published. Some writers do a lot of sorting, the trial-and-error stuff, in their head. Some who claim to do only one or two drafts will admit that their process has not always been that productive. Most writers' apprenticeships resulted in a great quantity of unpublished words. Many writers have simply forgotten how it was when they first began writing.

The writing-without-thinking system that I teach and advocate does tend to more digression, more unused (or unusable) words and pages than other, more disciplined approaches. But unless you already have a system for getting words on paper that satisfies you, the trial-and-error method will definitely work.

It will increase your output, increase your pleasure in the doing, increase possibilities, and ultimately lead to success. This route to success in writing appears to be a longer, less-traveled path, but the destination is often the same.

To invest time and energy in this kind of creative exploration is risky. You are taking the chance that the result will merely be a learning experience, which some people regard as failure. This is a difficult risk for most of us to undertake. We fear failure, and we fear being "failures."

Failure, however, is an event — not a person. I can fail to bring my story to a satisfying conclusion, and I can fail to get it published, but neither of those things alone makes me a failure. If I'm committed to learning from my experience with writing, from my trials and errors, then nothing is a failure — all is learning.

My failures, those efforts which did not result in satisfaction, were usually *much more powerful learning experiences* than those which succeeded.

For example, when I first began taking a writing class I thought I *should* write children's stories. After all, I had four children, and I was depriving them of my presence two nights a week to attend class. Therefore, if I wrote a story for each one of them, I could justify spending time and energy away from home.

Today's consciousness about motherhood is more enlightened, at least in the media. Nevertheless, I often encounter students, both men and women, who feel they need to justify their involvement with writing for similar reasons and in similar ways.

During my first weeks in class, I dutifully created a story for each of my children, which they seemed to enjoy. However, the stories were failures in my class, and failures in getting published. I wrote half a dozen of them before I realized that I really didn't know very much about being a child, about the playfulness of childhood. During my own early years, I had been rewarded for being serious. I became a pseudo-adult at an early age.

Recalling those stories now, I see why they didn't work. They were heavy on the moralizing, with an adult-parental consciousness rather than the more appropriate childlike point of view. And suitably enough, I certainly hadn't enjoyed the writing of them, but had considered them only a "duty."

So I failed in my goal of writing children's stories. I was not a failure, however. The time was not wasted, because I learned what I didn't want to write, and I pleased my children. (That was my real intention anyway. It would have been more useful to simply appreciate that and question my ambition to publish.) I learned that I need to write those things that are really important for me. I learned not to get sidetracked with my "I should write..." projects, those ideas which concern pleasing others in some way instead of pleasing myself.

WORDPLAY #10

Here are some useful questions to ask yourself before beginning a new writing project:

1. Who are you doing this for? Are you excited about it? Are you doing it primarily for yourself?

2. How important is it to explore these ideas on paper? Is it important to do this now?

3. Do you believe passionately in what you're writing?

4. Are you willing to explore this idea in writing to the best of your ability? Are you willing to invest time on a regular basis for this exploration?

5. Are you willing to let go of all expectations or demands of perfection or performance?

6. Are you willing to risk doing it no matter what?

7. Are you determined to enjoy either the success of your creative exploration or the opportunity for a rich learning experience?

If you answered "yes" to most of these questions, there's no way you can fail, no way you cannot find value in the trial-and-error-and-error-and-error method of writing.

17

Accessing Both Past and Future

A lthough writing is very much a here-and-now action, knowing how to release the past and use it appropriately can be helpful. Knowing how to capitalize on daydreaming and fantasies of the future can provide creative shortcuts for our efforts as well.

Here's a short essay, written in 1823 by Ludwig Borne, which still speaks clearly to today's would-be writer:

> There are men and books that teach Latin, Greek, or French in three days, and bookkeeping in only three hours. So far, however, no one has offered a course on How to Become a Good Original Writer in Three Days. And yet, it's so easy! There is nothing to learn, but plenty to unlearn; nothing to acquire, but much to forget. Every human mind is born with beautiful ideas — new ideas, too, since in every human being the world is created anew. But life and education write their useless stuff over them and cover them up.
>
> To see things as they really are, consider this: We know an animal, a fruit, a flower in their true shape; they appear to us the way they are. But would anyone

understand the true nature of a chicken, an apple tree,
or a rose if he knew only chicken pie, apple sauce, or
rose perfume? And yet that's all we ever get in the
sciences, and in anything that we take in through our
minds rather than our senses. It comes to us changed
and made up; we need to know it in its raw, naked form.
Thinking is the kitchen where all truths are killed, plucked,
cut up, fried, and pickled. What we need most today are
unthinking books — books with things in them rather
than thoughts.

There are only very few original writers. Our best
writers differ from the poorer ones far less than you might
think. One writer creeps to his goal, another runs, a
third hobbles, a fourth dances, a fifth drives, a sixth rides
on horseback: but the goal and the road are common to
all. Great new ideas are found only in solitude: but where
is solitude to be found? You can get away from people
— and at once you are in the noisy market-place of books;
you can throw away all the books too; but how do you
clear the mind of all the conventional ideas that education
has poured into it? The true art of self-training is the
art of making yourself ignorant: the finest and most
useful of the arts and one that is rarely and poorly
practiced.

The true search for knowledge is not like the voyage
of Columbus but like that of Ulysses. Man is born abroad,
living means seeking your home, and thinking means
living. But the home of ideas is the heart; if you want
fresh water, you must draw from the source; the mind is
but a river, on whose banks live thousands who muddy
its waters by washing, bathing, flax-steeping, and other
dirty business. The mind is the arm, the heart is the
will. Strength can be acquired, increased, and trained,
but what good is strength without the courage to use it?
A cowardly fear of thinking curbs us all; the censorship
of public opinion is more oppressive than that of govern-

ments. Most writers are no better than they are because they have ideas, but no character. Their weakness comes from vanity. They want to surpass their fellow writers, but to surpass someone you must meet him on his own ground, to overtake someone you must travel the same road. That's why the good writers have so much in common with the bad ones: the good one is like the bad one, but a little bit bigger; he goes in the same direction, but a little farther.

To be original you must listen to the voice of your heart rather than the clamor of the world — and have the courage to teach publicly what you have learned. The source of all genius is sincerity; men would be wiser if they were more moral.

And now comes the application that I promised: Take several sheets of paper and for three days in succession, without any pretense or hypocrisy, write down everything that comes to your mind. Write what you think about yourself, about women, about the Turkish War, about the Fonk Trial, about the Last Judgment, about your boss — and after three days you will be beside yourself with surprise at all the new, unheard-of ideas you had. That's the art of becoming an original writer in three days![1]

Some of the historical references are outdated, as well as statements that hint at the subordinate role of women; however, we can easily substitute the Vietnam War or today's headlines to bring us up to date. Borne's method, which Freud claims was the basis for psychoanalysis, is a simple and wise process for letting go of the past. It can also generate some ideas that are worth playing with which are part of your past experience.

"The true art of self-training," Borne calls it. That's all writing really is. It's certainly what my workshops and this book are all about. I hope you will take the time to follow his simple suggestions for "making yourself ignorant."

Now let's move from 1823 to the future — your future.

WORDPLAY #11

This is a fantasy of the future. Move yourself ahead mentally two years. What is the year, month, day? How old will you be then?

Write steadily. No thinking, no pausing. Write for exactly fifteen minutes. Set a timer if you need to.

Begin your writing with these statements: "It is (month/day/year). I am _____years old."

As you project yourself ahead two years in time, explore on paper your fantasy of what life might be like, or better yet, how you'd like your life to be. Where are you living? With whom? What changes have occurred in your life in the past two years? How are you feeling about those changes and about your life? *Write in the present tense. Write as if it were that date today and those things were happening now.* What are you doing that you've always dreamed of doing? What is your involvement with writing? Write anything you like, as long as you write as if it were happening today. Here's your chance to try on some of your dreams for size. This exercise works best if you approach it as a just-for-fun playful thing to do with words on paper.

Enjoy. Begin now.

Although this exercise is simply a projection into the future, it is also versatile: if you can see or imagine something happening, it's more likely to come true. This technique is a useful way to tap into your subconscious, bringing more things into your awareness.

The projection exercise can also be used to explore options. When confronted with a choice that you're unsure about, do a projection into the future for each option. Try out your decisions. *No thinking! See what happens on paper instead.* Write until something surprises you. You can pick any period of time, from the next few months to five years.

This approach can also be used to help you sort out ideas to write about, especially book, story, or article ideas. Fantasize that your book or story is complete. Fantasize about what will happen as a result of its completion. How do your friends and family feel about your success? Again, write until something surprises you.

This technique is also useful for probing and re-experiencing the past, any time in your past. Simply go back to the desired date or season of year (summer, Christmas, your tenth birthday) and be as specific as possible. *Write in the present tense, as if that time were now.* For example: "It is June 19 ___ . I am ____years old, and living at (address) in (city/state). The people (I'm living with) (in my life) are ___

_____ ."

Set down as many details about your surroundings as you can — your family, friends and other people, pets, the circumstances of your life. *Stay in the present tense.*

There's a profound difference in both the quality and quantity of output between that which is recollected ("I remember when") and that which is re-experienced ("It's my tenth birthday today and I hope I'm going to get a party"). Because memory is filtered through the critic, what Freud called "the censor of the mind," our recollections are often distorted. Those of you who have kept journals have probably noticed this when rereading them. Try this access to the past both ways, first through recollection, and then by re-experiencing it, just to prove the difference to yourself. Play around with this idea. When you imagine that something is happening now, in the present, your ideas flow from the creative and childlike part of you, the part that knows how to pretend. What is produced on paper as a result of this method will be neither totally accurate nor profound. But somewhere in the words and pages produced, hopefully, will be something you didn't know before, something useful. This is often discovered later, when reading over what has been written, rather than at the time of writing. It will be an insight, perhaps, or something interesting or amusing.

18

Where Do You Find the Time?

The most pertinent factor regarding writing time is best stated as follows: *people make room in their lives for what is important to them.*

Set aside a regular time for your writing, not necessarily on a daily basis, but certainly on a consistent basis. Even in my busiest weeks, my aim is to get forward motion on my current writing project during the week. I want to accumulate manuscript pages, "do something, even if it's wrong."

I set aside the time. As little as one-and-a-half hours a week will keep the momentum of the project going. And I make sure that time is spent writing — putting words on paper. Writing is a measurable endeavor, measurable in terms of pages or, better yet, word count.

Remember that three-part writing exercise at the end of Chapter Eleven? I hope you took the time to do it. If not, stop now and put words on paper for at least fifteen minutes. This next idea will be much more useful for you if you work from a personal point of reference.

Go back and count the number of words on your paper. Multiply that total by 365. This figure will give you the number of words you would have on paper if you wrote for that amount of time each day for a year. Usually the count runs well over 100,000 words. Only 350 words per day, for instance, when multiplied by 365, equals 127,750 words!

Most books published today run between 60,000 and 100,000 words — that's a typical size for a novel. Nonfiction and children's books may sometimes be less than 40,000 words. Even after applying the iceberg model to usable finished work (i.e., a large percentage gets thrown out or edited away), fifteen minutes a day could produce a significant number of final draft words in a year.

I frankly admit that this kind of writing often produces a very raggedy first draft — zero-draft stuff. However, fifteen minutes a day, even in the busiest life, *is* achievable. And if you are, indeed, putting words on paper that entire fifteen minutes, saving your thinking about it for the times before and after your daily writing period, then you'll end up with something that you wouldn't have otherwise achieved.

During those fifteen minutes, it really doesn't matter what you write as long as it's even vaguely related to the subject or idea you've chosen. All of the work will be useful in the sense that it will feed the work that follows. Your daily writing period will create the continuity, momentum and involvement that you want to begin with.

One of my students who had a fulltime job, a demanding social life, and family obligations was skeptical of the idea that fifteen minutes a day could produce anything of value, but she was willing to try it out for herself.

"I have forty-five minutes each weekday for lunch. It only takes me twenty minutes to eat. I'll write for fifteen minutes five days a week. My weekends belong to my family."

Every week, she brought into class the results of that writing. Often, her efforts were scrawled on the back of a lunchsack. The scenes from the novel she was writing, maybe one or two a week, sparkled with aliveness. Everyone was surprised, including me.

Anthony Trollope said, "A small daily task, if it be really daily, will beat the labors of a spasmodic Hercules." Trollope also said, "Three to four hours a day is as much as any writer needs to do if he is indeed writing during that time."

The output from this writing time will be different for each person, and the time it will take to complete a first or final draft is also an individual matter. To think only in terms of word or page count, however, may lead to feeling overwhelmed by the numbers. You may lose a sense of fun, of excitement and creativity. I used to feel I could never do a book, until I learned that a book was written just like anything else, one page at a time, and all I really had to concern myself with was today's page or pages. Those daily pages, that daily quota, however, was vital.

So, it is not a lot of time that's required at first, but a regular involvement with your writing on a week-to-week basis. As little as *one-and-a-half hours weekly will advance your dream of writing.* If you are using these short fragments of time, whether it's part of a lunch hour, or an hour-and-a-half on Sunday afternoon, it's vital to protect that time from intrusions and distractions.

For years I wrote at home, with a husband and four children underfoot. I finally got a separate room in my house for my writing, but they all traipsed in and out constantly, especially in the summertime. Though I often complained that my family didn't take my writing seriously, it took me a long time to admit that I hadn't taken it seriously enough to protect it properly. I seldom closed my office door. I never said, "Please don't interrupt me while I'm writing."

Annie Dillard was asked about her Pulitzer Prize-winning *Pilgrim at Tinker Creek.* Where did she find the time to write? After all, wasn't she a housewife? Her answer:

> *I don't do housework. Life is too short, and I'm too*

*much of a Puritan. If you want to take a year to write
a book, you have to take that year, or the year will take
you by the hair and pull you toward the grave. Let the
grass die. I let almost all of my indoor plants die from
neglect while I was writing the book. There are all kinds
of ways to live. You can take your choice. You can keep
a tidy house, and when St. Peter asks you what you did
with your life, you can say, I kept a tidy house, I made
my own cheese balls.*[1]

Although I never had that kind of dedication, I eventually learned that the question of time also includes the
factor of energy. Different tasks in writing need different
kinds of time and energy. Journal writing can be done on
demand, unless I am dealing with intense emotions, in
which case I need not only protected time, but privacy. First-
draft creative work needs "prime time," the maximum energy time of my day, the time I feel the freshest.

When I first began writing, I was a night person and I
wrote best late at night after the house was quiet. Later, I
used to write when the kids were down for a nap or at
school. Eventually, I found I needed to schedule my creative-
stage writing in the morning, before anything else claimed
my attention.

Medium-energy tasks, like rewriting or manuscript
typing, can be scheduled for afternoons or evenings. Some
days, I discovered, are low-energy days from the outset.
Those are the times I do filing and sorting and recopying,
but very little else. It's important to assess your energy level
when scheduling even small amounts of writing time, lest
you set yourself up for failure or disappointment.

Another factor to consider is your particular style for
getting things done. Are you a daily routine person, or a
deadline worker? If you are a binge artist, a wait-until-the-
last-minute-then-bang-it-out kind of person, it might be
more useful to plan a weekly writing binge or two, rather

than try for a more regular, and personally incompatible schedule.

Deadline workers are often very efficient, but usually suffer from what the world calls procrastination. Procrastination has a bad reputation and those who practice it usually feel guilty about it. If you normally put things off until the last minute, but always get the important things done, you need to stop feeling guilty and recognize that procrastination is a useful prioritizer for you. Don't try to change your style. Remember: *if it works, don't fix it!*

Also, if a writing schedule is a new habit for you, and you forget and miss a day or two, it's important not to think you have to do several days' writing all at once. If, for whatever reason, you miss a day, just skip it. There's no penalty, and you don't have to make it up.

Guilt interferes with the primary purposes of writing, which are fun, pleasure, and personal value.

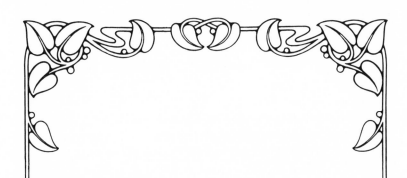

THE SEVEN LAWS OF WRITING

1. To write *is an active verb. Thinking is not writing.* Writing is words on paper.

2. Write passionately. Everyone has loves and hates; even quiet people lead passionate lives. Creativity follows passion.

3. Write honestly. Risk nakedness. Originality equals vulnerability.

4. Write for fun, for personal value. If you don't enjoy it, why should anyone else? Pleasure precedes profit.

5. Write anyway. Ignore discouraging words, internal and external. Persistence pays off.

6. Write a lot. Use everything. Learning comes from your own struggles with words on paper.

7. Write out of commitment to your ideas, commitment to yourself as a writer. Trust yourself.

PART FOUR

ANYBODY CAN
KEEP WRITING

19

Tracking an Idea

Right-brain/left-brain research is fascinating, increasingly complex, and even debatable. In summarizing this research, I've chosen not only to simplify (staying within the scope of this book), but also to stick with my own opinions, observations, and experience. The following list of right- and left-brain characteristics is an informal presentation of how the brain seems to handle the different tasks of writing.

In distinguishing between right- and left-brain functions, I've limited the list to include only those factors which I feel *strongly* influence the act of writing and the experience of writing, from the initial idea to the finished product.

Here's how what I call the "write-brain experience" happens:

RIGHT-BRAIN CHARACTERISTICS	LEFT-BRAIN CHARACTERISTICS
emotional	intellectual
sensory	speech
images/pictures	thoughts/judgments
primitive expression (beyond words)	precise language (reflecting learning)
simultaneous (Ah hah!) intuitive (insightful) creative	sequential logical (step-by-step) rational
synthesizing	analytical
fantasy (inner reality)	goals/planning (outer reality)
imaginative (seeing things happening)	evaluative (thinking things through)
fun/pleasure/freedom	duty/discipline
accepting (anything goes)	critical (questioning)
metaphor puns	abstract thought wit
spontaneity (no limits)	judgmental (controlling)
global/holistic (sees large picture)	focused (detail-oriented)
timelessness (no time recognition)	timekeeper (schedules/quotas)
receptive (perceives and processes visual information, inner and outer)	active (takes action/gets things done)
EXPERIENTIAL (visual/sensory/emotional)	**CONCEPTUAL** (ideas/constructs)

I have noticed that my writing students seem to fall into two categories:

1. Those whose production of pages is small and labored. "Tight and constipated," as one man complained. Their writing is logical in concept, mechanically correct, but often sterile in feeling. These students are well-organized, excellent in the presentation of facts, and skill-oriented, but usually have difficulties writing fiction.

2. The others, usually a smaller group, tend to produce an abundance of pages. They love the process of writing, but have problems figuring out how to organize the pages or edit them into a logical, satisfyingly coherent whole. They frequently experience difficulties with outlines and factual data.

My advice to the first group, the "left-brain-dominant writers," is to put their rational/critical self aside, and let themselves go, loosen up. To write and write and write. My advice to the second group, the "right-brain-dominant group," is to build their skills by breaking down the job of organization, focusing on small tasks that allow them to develop a sense of discrimination between what serves their story and what is extraneous and needs to be left out.

Good writers, successful writers, writers who experience satisfaction in their writing, need both right- and left-brain competence. Many highly successful writers do this unconsciously, or develop this faculty to the point where there's a free flow between the use of their left and right brains as they work on writing and developing their ideas and books.

One contention about the right brain is that it is non-verbal, having nothing to do with words and language, and therefore is not an appropriate place from which to begin an act that concerns itself intensively with words and language. My own experience, and that reported by my students, appears to be that the right brain seems to have language, but the words tend to be primitive, the vocabulary unsophisticated.

That's one of the main reasons most of us are unhappy with our first drafts. The right-brain influence results in crude verbal expression (although the emotional tone will be true). The left-brain role is to rewrite and add precision of language and clarity of thought.

With right-brain dominance, there's an image-rich fluidity, a sense of flow, of oneness with the material. And, frequently, a lack of precision when the words are first put on paper. Practice is required to combine fluidity with the precision that finished writing needs, and this precision comes with the experience of doing it over and over and over again, using left-brain discrimination. It's a gradual learning experience.

I used to feel frustrated because I couldn't understand how it was that I knew the principles of good writing intellectually, yet couldn't produce pages which reflected that knowledge. I thought there was something wrong with me until I finally realized that there is always a time gap between my intellectual perception of a technique and my ability to execute it at will — when what I know in my head will come out my arm and hand and pen and consistently show up on paper.

The fine tuning of an idea happens when precision and fluidity become integrated. When right and left brains work together, there's an easy back and forth process of refinement. The write-brain experience happens when the two work in harmony with each other.

RIGHT   LEFT

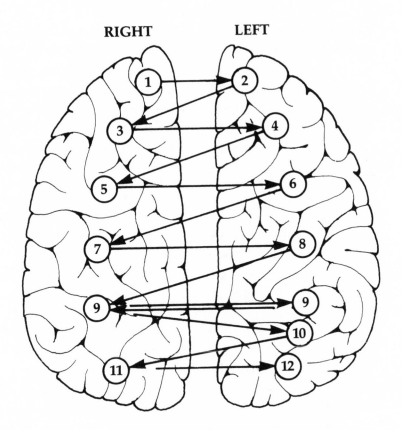

TRACKING AN IDEA

1. "Wow! What a great idea." (Idea spark + intuitive connection = excitement.)

2. Acknowledgement — "Sounds like a possible book." Makes notes on back of envelope.

3. Fingerpainting with words — playing around with the bits and pieces, feeding energy into it. Pleasurable feelings. Language fuzzy, primitive. (Nonlinear doodling.)

4. Organizes ideas/notes. Makes list of tasks, sets time schedule. Decides to do it. (Linear development.)

5. Explores sensory/emotional/imaginative possibilities of idea. High creativity/excitement. Sees things happening.

6. Reads over notes/pages. Commits to finish first draft.

7. More sprawling mass of words on paper. Making connections. Generating surprises with raw material. Zero draft. Eventually runs out of energy.

8. Evaluates sprawling first draft. Decides it's worth the long-term investment of time to rewrite. Makes suggestions for changes. Gives directions for rewrite. Rearranges material in a logical form (uses scissors and tape). Imposes structure.

9. Rewriting/rewriting/rewriting (an ongoing collaboration between right and left brains).

10. Decides it's time to edit. Ruthlessly cuts away the "deadwords," the digressions. Removes anything which does not serve the idea/book. Upgrades language for precision.

11. Looks at the book as a whole. "How does it feel?" Is it satisfying? Are the elements/parts in balance? If not, brainstorm about what to do.

12. Organizes a final typing. Polishing/fine tuning of book. Uses dictionary to check spellings/definitions.

And, if the book is to be marketed, hopefully to be published, the left brain researches publishers and devises a strategy. The right brain aids in "Creative Marketing," often with outrageous ideas, especially for promotion. The left brain implements the ideas and carries them through to completion.

20

Lights, Camera, Action

Focus on the writer (close-up shot): Writer paces floor. Looks preoccupied, but smiles to self from time to time. Finally chuckles aloud, rummages around for a pen that works, locates a spiral notebook that's hardly been used. Sits down to write. Scribbles a few sentences. Stares into space. Frowns. Leaps to feet. Resumes pacing. Jots things down in notebook mid-stride. Sits at desk. Begins to write in earnest. Looks up an hour-and-a- half later. Can't believe how late it's gotten.

A lot of things happen when we sit down to write. That part of us that has gotten us to the desk at a certain time says, "Sit down. Sit still. Get to work. You've got to write your 500 words today. Hurry up. Settle down. Stop fiddling around." This is the voice of the taskmaster.

The part of us that needs (and wants) to do the creative first draft, or zero draft, tends to resist sitting still, resists orders, resists anything that sounds like work. It's a very youthful, exuberant part of us, usually excited or intensely curious, fascinated by just about everything. It wants to express its excitement in words on paper, but is often impatient with the time it takes, or with having to sit in one place for very long. This creative child wriggles and fidgets and paces.

However, once it gets started, it gets so absorbed in the activity, in the playground of paper, ideas, and words, that it totally loses track of time. The experience is everything; it feels good, and nothing else exists for that space of time. It often hates to put the writing aside for the intrusions of eating or sleeping.

Original writing, the first draft of anything, ends up being a collaboration between the taskmaster and the creative child. The taskmaster takes care of logistics. First, it organizes the time. Then, if it has enough discipline over its need to control, it bows out for the sake of the end product.

The taskmaster must voluntarily surrender to the chaos of the fun-loving creator, who doesn't do things in a linear, logical way. This creator just scatters words around with a crude vitality. The intelligent taskmaster, however, knows that crude vitality is the magic ingredient. Realizing it can't *think* that dimension into the writing, it lets go, knowing that later it will have the opportunity to run quality-control on the job as a whole.

People who claim they can write only when they're inspired are those who wait for the child to get excited in the presence of paper and pencil. The intelligent taskmaster has learned that the child will write at prearranged times (on schedule) if it is allowed to do its fretting and wriggling on paper. Taskmaster stands guard over the time, whether fifteen minutes or three hours. It has set up the kind of schedule appropriate for getting the pages done. Then it lets the child roam free, in essence saying: "Here's your paper and pencil. Do whatever you want. I'll let you know when you can go outside."

The child will squirm and fret, but will eventually settle in to have fun with whatever is at hand. As it begins to play with the words, it sprawls stuff out, often in a brainstorming, nonlinear, doodling way. Maybe one-tenth will be usable, but it's a vital tenth, and the proportion of good stuff to digressive output is normal and natural.

Mark Harris, writer and teacher, said:

> *Writing comes very hard to me. I do not understand why people think writing is easy.... I am at a loss to know how to arrive at Word One, much less the whole piece.... Seeking a first line, I pound the typewriter very fast to start with, not for speed but for structure and discovery.... I cut in on my facts at any point, haphazard, confident that something will lead to something and eventually to a beginning, by which time the work I've done up ahead will inform the work behind.... Begin anywhere.... Most beginning writers cannot go forward because they insist on making every sentence clean before going on to the next. Somehow I learned to live with the chaos of a first draft.*[1]

D.T. Suzuki, the Zen master, stated it even more simply. "Cultivate in yourself a good similarity to the chaos of the universe surrounding you."

Chaos is one challenge, boredom another. Many writers report stages of feeling so bored with their book or project that they end up postponing, prolonging, or abandoning the project. Forward movement ceases.

One definition of boredom caught my eye recently. I was driving past the corner gas station. Its readerboard announced: *Boredom is rage spread thin.*

That certainly is my experience. When the excitement is gone, it feels like I've just awakened from a dream, wondering, "Where am I?" I look at what I've produced. I think, "What is this that I've been wasting my time on?" Then I feel enraged, duped, discouraged. I want to tear up everything I've done and throw it away.

F. Scott Fitzgerald said, "Boredom is not an end product — it is, comparatively, rather an early stage in life and in art. You've got to go by, or past, or through boredom, as through a filter, before the clear product emerges." And Irving Wallace said, "Starting to write a new book — especially the first few pages, before I get to know the characters, bores me. After fifty pages, the tedium wears off."

So the antidote to boredom, like many of the difficulties associated with writing, is to acknowledge it in your prewriting "dump," and then keep going until you break through to another level of excitement, of creativity, of surprise.

Emotional authenticity creates appropriate and satisfying surprises for the reader and often for the writer as well. It's important to distinguish between *concept* and *experience* to achieve this authenticity. Read through the following zero drafts of the same incident.

First Version: Two months ago, a friend of mine killed himself. He commited suicide. I found myself at first feeling responsible for what had happened to him. Wondering what I could have done differently. Finally realizing that I could only be responsible for myself. That it was an illusion that I really could have done anything to keep him from doing what he did. I had to free myself of the expectations that I could have saved him, or could play rescuer to save his widow from her pain. But all I could do was to deal with my own feelings of loss, go through my own grieving process.

Second Version: A friend of mine killed himself about two months ago. He parked by the side of the road near his house and put a bullet through his head. A phone call woke me in the middle of the night — a mutual friend who knew I cared about Bob. I wanted to rush right over. To do something. To comfort the friend who had called. But I just hung up the phone and crawled back into my sleeping bag feeling sick and lonely. I curled up into a ball and rocked myself back and forth. Kept thinking there was something I could have/should have done so Bob wouldn't have needed to do that. Somehow,

I'd let him down. And I was angry at him for going away, for doing that. I rocked myself a long, long time. I tried to comfort myself. I wondered what I could possibly say to Sue. I felt very lost and very alone. And I wanted not to feel so alone.

Notice the difference between *concept* in the first version, and *feeling* in the second one. The latter is closer to the direct experience and it avoids conceptual words like suicide, responsibility, illusion, expectation, loss, grieving process. Those are the kind of words which distance us, words which *explain* feelings rather than *share* experiences.

21

Collaborating with the Subconscious

Experiencing, feeling, and seeing are the essence of the right brain's influence. Many authors have mentioned, "I see things happening," or "movies run inside my head," as a way of explaining the source of their inspiration. According to Annie Dillard:

> But there is another kind of seeing that involves a letting go. When I see this way I sway transfixed and emptied. The difference between the two ways of seeing is the difference between walking with and without a camera. When I walk with a camera I walk from shot to shot, reading the light on a calibrated meter. When I walk without a camera, my own shutter opens, and the moment's light prints on my own silver gut. When I see this second way I am above all, an unscrupulous observer.[1]

Most attempts to explain the right-brain experience fall short because it is always a personal, emotional happening. Words simply are inadequate to explain right-brain functioning, and *your* experience of the same state may *feel* different anyway. For most novelists and poets, it's familiar territory. For others, it's a foreign country.

My first encounter — as an adult and a writer — with that rich visual realm inside my own head was deliberately planned. One spring, I'd been playing in fits and starts with an idea for a book based on my adventures as a divorcee.

I began several first chapters, outlined a nonfiction approach, and developed fictional characters for a semi-autobiographical novel. Then I tried it as an advice book, sharing what I'd learned along the way. Going back to the novel form, I tried it in the first person, then the third person. The work did not progress either way. My self-imposed, zero-draft schedule wasn't working either.

I obviously didn't feel that sense of commitment so necessary to completing a viable first draft. Judging by my results on this project, something essential was missing.

At that time, I was living a very complex and intense life, full of daily involvement with words. I was doing many writing workshops, preparing written work as handouts. I had a great deal of verbal interaction with my students, such as lecturing, evaluating manuscripts, and helping them to rewrite. I was writing daily in my own journal, making lists and notes for stories I had neither the time nor energy to develop.

I was talking a lot. In class and socially. Talking. Talking. Talking.

The rest of the time I read: student manuscripts, non-fiction for information, and mysteries for pleasure and escape, to unwind from all the serious stuff (like earning a living and getting over a passionate and painful love affair).

I decided that what I really needed was a vacation — a vacation from words. The only way to achieve clarity, to focus on an idea for my novel-to-be, was to get unhooked from words; a temporary divorce, of sorts.

My plan was to go camping for six days, by myself. I would take no written material. No books, magazines, manuscripts, notes, or paper to write on. Not even my journal (a painful decision, as it had been my companion and solace for nearly twenty years). No pens. No pencils. No newspapers.

Further, I would avoid talking to anyone during those six days. I would risk being alone with myself and my very busy eight-track head. I was willing to risk what might happen to this compulsive reader/writer/talker without any of the usual outlets for that energy.

I located a state park on an island not too far away, a place both reasonably safe and remote. I borrowed a camper to sleep in, packed the bare minimum of food and supplies, and drove off for my solitary adventure, totally prepared to allow myself the craziness of withdrawal from the world of words. I would be waiting to see what emerged, trying to make myself new, in a sense. In the process of courting an idea for my novel that was different from the ones I'd already accumulated, I found myself in search of a more direct route to my subconscious.

It was mid-May and unusually decent weather for the Pacific Northwest. After a two-hour drive from my house — a causeway my only link to the mainland — I parked near a grove of fir trees on the edge of an old apple orchard. The Olympic Mountains were visible to the west. The rocky beach of Jarrel's Cove was a two-minute walk from my campsite.

The afternoon, sunny but not too warm, stretched interminably before me. I looked around. There was nothing to do. Nothing to read. No paper. No pencil. Nothing to do but walk. So that's what I did.

I walked several miles along the beach, down to the point and back. Walked around the roads a while, then returned to camp, built a fire, and cooked a simple dinner the hard way. It took longer that way, and I seemed to have plenty of time. No evening newspaper. No manuscripts to read. After dinner, I walked the beach again, more slowly this time. I returned late, my sweater pockets full of sand dollars, pretty colored rocks from the beach, and bits of driftwood. I arranged them in a pleasing pattern on a slab of wood and crawled into my sleeping bag, exhausted.

I awakened at daylight to the sounds of crows in raucous chorus, or argument. I couldn't sleep anyway — my head was overactive. So I got up, dressed, and ate, all by 6:30, definitely not the norm for me.

What to do? No list of things-to-do-today. No journal to write in. No letters to answer. I found it hard to sit still without paper of some sort in my hands. The extent of my addiction became clearer. I wanted a book, a manuscript, my spiral notebook, scratch paper — anything.

I began walking and exploring more of the island. I encountered a deer; watched two kingfishers dip and screech and circle the sound. Found a heavily forested piece of property with a weathered "For Sale" sign — old cedar trees, a meadow with sweeping views of both the mountains and the sound.

A perfect place for a writers' colony. I sat and daydreamed a while. Then, restless, I walked and walked and walked. I must have walked six to eight hours that day. (An hour or two was my usual habit.) Finally, I took off my watch and put it in the glove compartment of my car.

Over the next few days, I cooked my meals slowly. The ache for my notebook, something to write on, something to read, diminished, but never disappeared. I returned from frequent walks with more rocks and bits of flotsam. Each evening, I arranged and rearranged my growing collection on the slab of wood.

With nothing to do, nobody to talk to, nothing to read, my head did indeed go crazy. But I was no longer afraid of this craziness. I had often charted it in the pages of my journal. It was familiar, and although not always comfortable, it was not something that ever got bizarre enough to really worry about. The verbal deprivation didn't change its nature, it just intensified. I've always conversed with myself! My journal, my other writings, and my talking had been safety valves.

I noted mentally that on the first day I'd covered a lot of ground during my walks, but hadn't really noticed very much of what was around me. Day two: did lots of walking and saw more, but not in great detail. Day three: I slept a lot, exhausted from the extra walking. I saw a greater richness of colors, but the fresh air seemed to dull my mind. I couldn't remember what I was doing there...just that I had to stay. The day was drizzly, foggy. I felt foggy, too, and napped in between short walks.

Day four: I finally mellowed out. Enjoyed the lack of routine, the freedom from the demands of telephone and children and classes. I dawdled in the sunshine, strolled around. Saw everything in minute detail. Played with my bits of colored rock, sorting them according to color and size, assembling a kind of crude mosaic. Enjoyed the varied hues and textures. Like the button box of my childhood, it was totally absorbing.... Until I found myself feeling bored and discouraged, trying to remember my purpose for being there. The outdoor experiences were interesting, good source material for future books, as background, maybe.

I tried to remind myself that the main reason for taking this time out of my busy life was to find a new approach for my novel, but concentration on the idea was difficult. I preferred to play with my pretty rocks and couldn't seem to focus on my problems with writing. Nothing productive was happening.

On the afternoon of the fifth day, I gave up and decided to go home early the next morning, earlier than I'd planned. I felt like I'd blown it; once again, a victim of unrealistic expectations. I felt more than a little foolish.

An hour later, I was sitting under a tree in the apple orchard listening to the intermittent chirping of some baby birds. I could hear them clearly, but couldn't spot the nest. Warm sunshine bathed my face. I watched as a starling swooped away from a gnarled and twisted apple tree nearby. I noticed its leaves greening, but no blossoms yet. The starling returned, her beak full. She perched near a cleft in the tree, then dropped the worms. A loud and furious chirping ensued. She swooped away again.

Curious, I kept circling the tree, but still couldn't locate the nest. I drew back to watch more carefully. The mother bird, more cautious now, kept stopping to look my way. Finally, she darted in, dropped the food, and flew off again. I approached the tree, as the starling scolded from a distance. I stood on tiptoe and was able to see the baby birds through a knothole. The center of the tree had a natural, protected hollow, not visible from below. Excited, I watched their scrawny necks stretching skyward, hungrily searching, loudly cheeping.

I backed off. The mother bird bawled me out, then resumed her pattern of feeding. I wandered around the orchard, bemused by the sight of the baby birds, and fascinated by the fact that it had taken me four days to see something that was less than 100 feet from my campsite.

Suddenly, in my mind's eye, I saw a woman moving through an apple orchard. It wasn't me. It was someone I'd never met, never even seen before. I could see her vividly. And I could also see through her eyes and knew what she was thinking, what her background was; I knew her life experiences and knew the story she had to tell.

And I knew that her story would use all the stuff from my life, all those adventures I'd wanted to use in a novel. But they would be somehow transmuted, so they would not really be mine. They would be subtly changed, and fully hers.

That scene was so rich, so vivid in my mind, that I needed no pencil, no paper. I knew I wouldn't forget it, never forget her. And I knew that there would be time to begin the writing of it. I was struck by the fact that only an hour earlier I'd given up thinking I'd find an idea for my book. Yet, there I was, pregnant "with book."

The idea and the character and the voice for the novel were different from anything I'd done on paper before. Different from anything I'd ever *thought up*, or tried to *think up*.

In some way, I'd let go, given up, and then for perhaps the first time I had experienced that rich inner source of fiction I'd heard so many novelists speak of so glibly. I now had tangible evidence that I could actively collaborate with my subconscious. Now that I recognized what it felt like to experience creativity, I could consciously seek out and do those things that paved the way, that made it more likely to occur.

HOW TO ACTIVATE THE CREATIVE MODE

1. Precede writing time with thirty minutes or more of rhythmic, sustained exercise: running, walking, swimming, or biking.

2. Precede writing time with any meditation/relaxation process (Transcendental meditation, Zen meditation, Autogenics, self-hypnosis).

3. Visualize yourself (see yourself) enjoying writing just before you drift off to sleep at night.

4. Write early drafts by hand. Or, if you're a good typist, try freeflow writing in a darkened room. (Darken the screen on your word processor.) No peeking. Or shut your eyes while you type.

5. Use a spiral notebook for your project. Enter "thinking" notes on the left-hand pages. Save the right-hand pages for the strange, nonlinear offshoots. (The "what-ifs," the speculations.)

6. Remove your watch and keep clocks out of view. Set a timer (out of sight) if you need to control duration.

7. *Write without thinking/without stopping.*

HOW TO IDENTIFY THE CREATIVE MODE

1. Losing track of time. Sense of timelessness. Absorbed in the doing.

2. Feeling of pleasure, fun, delight, joy. Spontaneity.

3. Absence of self-consciousness. If you're analyzing, trying to figure out if you're there, you're not! It's only after the fact that you realize that's where you've been.

4. Total feeling of the here-and-now. No thought of past or future. No sense of outcome. Just oneness with the act of writing, the flow of words.

5. Nondiscriminating. No sense of right/wrong, good/bad distinctions or judgments. All is equal.

22

Shaping to Form

O nce the mass of raw material has been generated, the logical, critical mode (left brain) takes over. That take-over is called rewriting. It's been said that "easy reading means hard writing." In truth, easy reading means lots of rewriting, taking that haphazard mass of raw material and shaping it to form.

Content/idea is more important than form, but form cannot be neglected if the material is intended for anyone else to read. Often, writers will try to impose a more-or-less standard form upon their material, in an effort to "do it right."

The best approach for rewriting is an attitude of discovery, seeking to discover the inherent form in each piece within the sprawling rough draft. To chip away (edit out) anything which doesn't serve the idea. Or to build up: add specific examples, more precise language, flesh out skeletal impressions.

There are two essential questions you can ask which will help to focus the rewrite. The first is the question of intention. It's a self-interview process, best done in writing.

Ask yourself: "What is my intention for writing this? Or rewriting this? Why this story or subject? And finally, "What started me thinking about this idea? Where did it begin for me? Why is it important for me to write this? Why is this the best time?"

This process evolved from class discussions about pieces that felt fuzzy or off track. I'd keep asking questions until the writer came up with the real reasons for doing a particular piece. Invariably, the answers provided information that belonged in the writing itself.

The second essential question to consider concerns the audience. Ask yourself: "Who am I writing this for?" This is crucial, especially if you're writing for a wider audience than yourself.

Students tend to generalize and say: "For people over forty...for kids...for 'Playboy' or 'Redbook' or 'Guideposts'." They usually want as wide an audience as possible.

Aiming for a wide audience often results in a fuzzy focus. The solution is to think of a specific individual, someone you know or have known personally, and write or rewrite with that person firmly in mind. This approach can help you decide what to expand or what to leave out. Try this idea the next time you write.

It's useful to break the rewrite process down into more specific tasks, to think of it as a series of steps to be taken one at a time, rather than something that happens all at once.

The rewriting process is similar to the process of rock polishing. After my island vacation from words, a friend noticed that my box of rocks and pebbles (the ones I'd arranged and rearranged) looked dull and lusterless until they were put in a dish of water, when they came alive with color. My friend gave me a rock-grinding kit and I began polishing rocks just for fun.

Rock polishing has four major steps. The first is the

rough, or coarse, grind. The chosen rocks are placed in a hard rubber barrel along with coarse metal filings and water. They tumble, nonstop, for ten days or more. The tumbling, grinding action is similar to what happens at the beach — and the rough edges are eventually worn down. This stage is the longest of the four and, like the first stage of rewriting, it can't be hurried.

Depending on how uneven the surface of the rock (or how crude the expression of the idea), this stage may need to be repeated to achieve the desired results. Some rocks don't polish well no matter how long they are tumbled. Some ideas need to be discarded or abandoned as well.

The second stage is the fine grind, a more refined grinding that clears away further imperfections and roughness. The rocks are rinsed and sorted, then returned to the barrel with fine metal filings to tumble for a week or more. Some rocks, especially those from ocean beaches, are so smooth to begin with that I can start with the fine grind. Some writings are like that, too — not many, but some.

The third stage is the pre-polish, a shorter smoothing where the surface is readied for the polishing. The rocks tumble in a pumice-like slurry. Flaws often become visible during this stage and flawed rocks must either be returned to repeat an earlier stage, or discarded. Similar treatment is necessary for any writing that does not come up to standard.

The fourth and often final step is the polishing, where the rocks tumble in a solution of jeweler's rouge and water. In writing, this is where I type the final draft, dictionary by my side, checking as I go.

Processing one batch of rocks can take three weeks or longer. When I've completed the final step of the process, I usually feel excited. With keen anticipation, I rinse off the red polishing compound and view the results, my pretty pebbles, my jewels. I delight in the colors and markings. As I check them over, I notice that some, though beautiful, are still flawed. Some look better than I'd suspected they might.

Some are smooth, but not shiny like the rest, too soft to have anything but a matte finish.

My ideas and the rewriting process produce similar results, surprises and disappointments. It took me several months to get the hang of choosing the best pieces to polish, and years to learn to choose the better ideas to work on. Eventually, I did get better at selecting those which show the most promise of ending up relatively unflawed.

Unexpected problems *can* arise. Sometimes the power went off during the rock processing, stopping the tumbler in mid-cycle. Because I didn't catch it for a while, the resulting rocks were often uneven, lacking uniform luster. Occasionally they were unsalvageable. Likewise, if my writing gets interrupted for too long, I lose momentum, and sometimes the excitement I need to get through the first draft.

Each stage of rewriting has a different focus for me. The overriding concern, during the whole rewrite process, is clarity and good communication. Both of these are a result of respect for the reader, whether editor or friend. Each writing project has different demands. Some are more complex than others. Fiction seems to require more rewrites than nonfiction, for instance. The final stage is the one in which good spelling, punctuation, grammar, sentence structure, and paragraphing must be thoroughly addressed.

Knowing how to spell accurately is a quirk. It has nothing to do with intelligence or higher education. If you're truly a poor speller, it's best to hire an intelligent typist for the final draft, a naturally good speller who will correct your misspellings.

Punctuation is simply an aid to the reader, telling him when to pause, when to breathe, what words or phrases are most important. All the rules of both punctuation and grammar can be broken, or severely bent, *if* the result is clear and readable.

The only criterion when writing for a wider audience is: *does it work?* Does it communicate appropriately with the intended audience? Is it clear? Does it evoke the response you want from the reader? And, most important, is it satisfying for the reader?

23

The Write-brain Experience

Most of us have difficulty in knowing when to collaborate with our subconscious, and when it's time to start shaping our piece into good form. It takes a great deal of practice to feel comfortable and in command of our own creativity and skills.

It is necessary to become familiar with our individual two-stage process and make friends with whatever we find there. The following three-part writing experience is designed to help achieve understanding, cooperation, and synthesis between our right- and left-brain personae. It will help us learn to operate the "write-brain connection" that will aid in accomplishing our goals and dreams of writing.

This writing experience requires more time and energy than most of the others in this book. Set aside at least half an hour. A light-hearted, playful spirit is helpful, just as with all the other *Wordplay* exercises.

Hopefully, by this time, you will have a sense of the split betwen the creative and critical sides of you. It is helpful to give each side a name; choose words that feel right to you. Some names that students have used for the right-brain part of themselves are: Creator, Child, Funlover, Day-dreamer. Often a nickname, or the diminutive of your given name, works well. For instance, Jeanie is that creative, ex-cited part of me. My words for the left-brain part include: Critic, Teacher, Taskmaster, Watchdog, Quality Controller, Clyde.

WORDPLAY #12

1. Personify your left brain, using the projection tech-nique. Call it by the name you've given it. Treat it as if it were alive, a separate entity. Allow it to tell you about itself on paper. Enter into the spirit of this. Pretend you are the left brain, the part that loves to define and explain, so give it a chance to do that. Use the first person point of view. "I am Taskmaster, Jean's critical self...." Allow it to tell you about its education, its skills, its abilities, its preferences. Let it talk about the things it's good at, or the kind of things that make it uncomfortable.

Write without thinking. Write without stopping.

Begin now.

2. Now repeat this process for the creative side of you. First name it, then become it on paper. Allow it to express itself fully. The right-brain part appreciates freedom and fun and movement. Let it tell you where it operates in your life. What it likes. What it dislikes. It tends to be unsophisticated in expression, and may use slang and childlike language. It is often excitable, emotional. Use the first person. "I am Jeanie, the creative part of Jean. I like to dance. To play with words." *Write without thinking. Write steadily.*

Begin now.

3. After both sides have had a chance to fully express themselves, set up a conversation between them on paper. Ask them to talk about how each of them can help you get your writing done. Let them work out together how each

will make a contribution to your dreams about writing. Ask them to be specific. Find out who will help you get started, who will keep you going, and how that will be done. If either of them has fears or considerations about the other's role, now is the time to talk about it, to work it out, to come to some sort of agreement. Sometimes, at first, the best that can happen is that they agree to disagree.

You, the whole writer, can ask questions, but it's best to allow them to do most of the talking. Keep going with this until you feel a sense of completion, surprise, or satisfaction. If this doesn't happen the first time you do it, don't give up the idea. *Try at least three times.* Often, each writing experience using this format will be suprisingly different.

Once you've established a reasonably friendly relationship with these two parts of you, it's possible to use them as a resource, to summon them up at will, and ask them for help or guidance with any writing difficulty.

This is something that you must prove for yourself. I've never known it to fail when there's a willingness to try it with an open mind. Problems arise when expectations are too high and when the spirit of playfulness is missing. Skepticism, on the other hand, can't hurt, if you also have the willingness to do the exercise, just for the fun of it.

No thinking. No stopping.

Begin now.

24

Can Anybody
Get Published?

To get published nowadays, it's not enough that a piece of writing be both well-written *and* interesting. Now it has to have something more. That "something more" can be a matter of timing, transcendence, or both.

It has often been said that the secret of getting published is to have the right manuscript on the right desk at the right time. The writer can only make sure that his or her written effort is as well-done and professional as possible, and persist in keeping it circulating, so that it's always on somebody's desk (other than the writer's).

Timeliness can be determined by recognizing a rising trend or fad, or a social or media development. In the early eighties, the state of the economy generated dozens of "how-to-survive" nonfiction books. World crises and conflicts became the background for many best-selling suspense novels. The harsh realities of inflation at home and political unrest elsewhere made romance novels a sought-after form of escape.

The timing of a book is not that predictable. From the time you begin writing to the final completion of the project can be a matter of months, or even years; hence, timeliness alone is seldom the denominator of success. Something more is required.

Transcendence is an elusive quality, hard to define, but a quality that most good editors recognize. One editor said, "I know what I'm looking for when I see it in front of me." So much for asking an editor to tell you what he or she wants!

Transcendence is often that unique synergistic connection between the subject matter and the writer, the kind of connection that results in the product being greater than the sum of its parts. (A mathematical equivalent would be when one-plus-one equals three — or more. Or, a man plus woman results in one child, a third entity.)

Transcendence usually arises out of personal conviction or passion: the essential being of the writer is invested in the work. A clear intention, plus a sense of your audience, coupled with a sense of necessity that you, the writer, share this in written form, set the stage for transcendence. It is a quality which evolves from interaction with the subject. It can seldom be plotted or planned, or it will feel contrived to editors and readers alike.

The New Yorker called transcendence "the third reality" in its "Talk of the Town" column:

> *The characteristics that can create the third reality are, many of them, ineffable and unnamable. One that is instantly recognizable, however, and may even be a requirement, is care, without which high quality is unattainable. Care is itself an artistic statement that expresses love. For example, a novelist who chooses compassion for his subject but then draws his characters sloppily really expresses contempt. On the other hand, a novelist who writes about underworld violence but takes the time and expends the energy to bring his characters, good and bad, into being performs an act of love, a gratuitous act of caring, which stirs love in the*

reader as well and becomes the true statement — one could even say action — of the novel.

The ability of the novel to uncover the sanctity of every person, no matter how debased, and also to reveal the miraculousness, the preciousness of the humblest details of life is what makes the writing and reading of novels a humanistic enterprise of great importance: not just the creation and enjoyment of a diversion — though it can be just that — but acts to which one can appropriately bring one's most serious thoughts about life. [1]

What are your most serious thoughts about life? If you had just six months to live, what would you write? What do you know to be true? Your subjects, themes, and ideas need to be special, and so important to you that no other living person could write that piece in just that way. Your writings, fiction or nonfiction, must integrate your uniqueness with your story or topic.

If you are writing something that anybody else could write in the same way, let them do it. Choose those projects (or let them choose you) that have what one editor called "the thumbprint of the author."

Your books, ideas, and stories need to be personal as well as universal — where your experiences and your visions are honored. Your commitment to your ideas, your vision, needs to be intensely personal. When the value is in the doing, first and foremost, not just in the desire for an audience, then transcendence is more likely to occur.

Style may be a part of what transcendence is about, since style simply *is* the writer. To write with "style" simply means to write truthfully. To write honestly, not to impress, but to express a conviction, to express your creativity, or just to entertain; these are the attributes of style.

For the reader, the quality of transcendence manifests itself in evoking a response. An "Aha!" response, when the reader experiences surprise; "Yeah!" when the feeling is profound satisfaction or appropriateness. Not in a predictable way, however.

That's the impact which a good poem makes. James Dickey, a poet and novelist, said that what he wanted in a poem was, "...a fever. A fever and a tranquility." Opposites. Maybe transcendence is about the juxtaposition, and the compatibility, of opposites. Surprise! A sense of paradox, and a sense of acceptance and delight in that paradox. Here's the dictionary's definition:

Transcendent: 1. going beyond ordinary limits; surpassing; exceeding. 2. superior or supreme.

Can anybody get published?

If they want it badly enough, I believe they can, *if* they have the strong desire, the willingness to serve their apprenticeship, the ability to work hard with a dedication to professionalism, a sense of their own uniqueness, a belief in themselves, and an exuberant (or dogged) persistence.

Two things I look for which determine success in publication are: persistence, which includes determination and hard work, and an open mind, the willingness to learn about oneself from those who read your work and from your own struggles with words on paper.

25

Never Take Any Advice
You Don't Agree With

If you've ever taken an English class, you've probably
heard the advice, "Never end a sentence with a preposition." The title for this chapter and many sentences in this
book end with a preposition. Does that make them wrong?

Advice is a tricky thing. Most of us really don't want
advice. We seek approval, appreciation. We want to share
our ideas. David Frost said, "What a writer means by constructive criticism is a few thousand words of closely rea-
soned adulation."

I'm not sure I totally agree with that, but we writers
do need or want useful feedback at some point. We'll show
our writing to someone and say, "What do you think?" If
these people are our friends or relatives the response is
usually either congratulatory or devaluing.

"That's wonderful. Don't change a word. Send it out
to get published immediately." This response often sets up
unrealistic expectations. Reactions such as "That's rotten!"
or "You could do better," are often discouraging, especially
when the advice-giver proceeds to tell you in great detail

how they would have handled the idea differently (i.e., their way).

Very few people will ask you what kind of feedback you want, or attempt to discover what you were trying to communicate, or even reflect back on what they got from the reading.

Overencouragement or excessive praise can provide a momentary ego boost. And too many helpful suggestions can feel like an invalidation of our ideas or ourselves. It's difficult not to take criticism personally, especially since our writing is often intensely personal, either in content or in our investment of time and energy.

We need to be involved with our writing, yet not over-identify with it, when we solicit or accept reader response. The paradox is that our writing needs to be *intimately of us, but separate from us.* We need to cultivate an interested detachment to effectively use feedback or advice. We also need to filter out the possible bias of anyone from whom we ask advice.

We need to trust ourselves and our instincts. Otherwise, we try to take all the advice we're given, and our ideas get mangled or killed. We think others know more than we do but that's not necessarily true.

Writing is an act of faith in yourself and your vision. Works in progress are usually highly vulnerable, and it's important to develop a feel for the degree of your own vulnerability and the vulnerability of your work. Pay attention to what feeds and nurtures your writing, so you can ask appropriately for what you need. And discover how to effectively communicate what you don't need as well.

What you do need to develop for yourself is a kind of ruthlessness, so you can reject any comments that don't serve your writing, or that you don't really understand, or that simply don't feel good to you.

Even the best advice is of no value if it's inappropriate,

unappreciated, or misunderstood. You'll know you've gotten good advice when, after hearing it, your response is, "I wish I'd thought of that," or at least you find you have a healthy and genuine desire to try it out.

One of my students, new to writing, brought in the first chapter of a book and got a lot of varied suggestions for improvement. She returned to class the next week and announced, "I sorted the advice into three categories: (1) suggestions I understood and agreed with and felt I could do something about; (2) suggestions I understood and agreed with, but didn't know how to do; and (3) suggestions I either didn't understand or didn't agree with." That's a very useful sorting process and one I heartily recommend.

Any group of people in a writing class or elsewhere will offer advice. Everyone is a critic. However, only a few people in any given group will really have a sense of you, or of what you're trying to achieve or express. Therefore, you must learn to discriminate, to be ruthless in taking only the advice that you agree with. This also applies to advice from the instructor or leader.

All advice needs to be offered tentatively. All suggestions need to be taken with a grain of salt, if at all. It's useful to listen respectfully to all criticism offered. Never try to explain what you've written. Never defend. Never argue. There will usually be comments which are useful and others which are not. You are the one to decide which is which. Anybody or anything that discourages your belief in your writing or yourself, anything that inhibits your production of manuscript, is not constructive.

It is possible to learn something from almost everyone. Furthermore, there are professional readers that can be hired to review your work. If you want to write for publication, here are some ideas to think about before you get your manuscript evaluated. What are *your* questions?

Do you want to know: "Does my manuscript work? Is it satisfying for the reader? Is it appropriate for the intended audience? What are its strengths? What are its weaknesses? What do I need to do to make it publishable? Can you give me specific suggestions for improvement?"

Questions like these reflect a sense of apprenticeship, a willingness to revise under the guidance of a professional, and realistic expectations of what a successful manuscript evaluation can achieve. (Disappointment results from negative or vague questions like: "What's wrong with my writing? Do I have talent?") If you want to have your work professionally criticized, keep these points in mind.

BEFORE YOU PAY THAT READING FEE

1. Do your homework: All critics are not equal, or interchangeable, or useful *for you*. Ask around to find out who might be best for you.

2. Evaluate your evaluator: Get your questions answered beforehand. *Good rapport and mutual respect are essential.* Ask for references if you have any doubts.

3. Understand the nature of the beast: Evaluation is not a science. At best, *it's a helpful opinion based on experience and knowledge.* There are no rules regarding writing for publication that haven't been broken (which doesn't mean that rules and guidelines aren't useful).

4. Know what you want: Do you want feedback on form, or content, or both? Do you want encouragement, or help with idea development? (If you just want your grammar and punctuation cleaned up, an intelligent typist might be all you need.) Do you prefer a written critique, or an in-person consultation? Sometimes, the chance to ask questions can clarify criticism. (Consultations can be tape-recorded.)

5. Understand that you're in charge: You're the writer, the creator, the expert on your own work. It's your by-line that will appear on the published work.

Never take any advice that you don't agree with!

YOU ARE THE WRITER

You are the writer, the spinner of tales, the story-teller, the descendant of Scheherazade. You are the writer, the quiet observer and recorder of life, a troubador of truth. You are the creator of fascinating stories and poems, articles and books.

You are wise and, at the same time, full of humor and joy. You are highly creative and comfortable with the process of writing, the chaos of a first draft. You are wise, not because of what you know, but because of how you understand what you know. You are always at the center, at the core of what is happening, and you always write from that center.

Your words, in final draft, are clear and luminous and penetrating. Your books and written works create visions, meanings, insights, and awareness that had not existed before. Your enjoyment of the process of writing sustains your endeavors.

Your books are easy to read; every sentence, every paragraph, every chapter is honed down to sheer simplicity and meaningfulness. Everything you write is clear and functional, invested with passion and purpose.

You are a powerful and positive influence on yourself and others. Your daily writing time leaves you feeling refreshed and energized, eager to return to your desk the next day.

You perceive everything with a sense of great wonder that illuminates your writing. This gift of communication through your writing makes life full and fulfilling for you. You experience many rewards from your involvement with writing.

You are the writer.

SATISFACTION GUARANTEE

I hereby guarantee that (your name) is a unique human being who can write. _____ has had interesting experiences to write about and has something to say. There is something important for _____ to learn from the experience of writing, and _____ has the ability to put it into words.

I also guarantee that the more _____ is willing to trust to write truly, to write regularly, the more improvement will occur, and the more satisfaction _____ will experience.

Jean Bryant
Freelance Writer, Freelance Teacher
and Freelance Human Being

ACKNOWLEDGEMENTS

The philosophy and techniques expressed in this book, especially the *Wordplay* sections, are free adaptations of what is commonly called New Age thought (that not-really-new overlap of psychological and metaphysical principles).

However, contemporary forms of gestalt and psycho-synthesis, for example, do reflect the creativity of their orig-inators and this book has benefited from their ideas. The Ludwig Borne essay was discovered in an out-of-print book by Rudolph Flesch titled *How to Make Sense.*

Special thanks go to John Enright of ARC Seminars who introduced me to the difference between concept and experience, to the pervasiveness of projection, and who proposed the radical notion that it was okay to earn a living doing something you really loved.

Thanks also to Maureen Woodcock, Ann Combs, Janet Burr, and Sally Hartley for friendship and honest feedback. To my children, Richard, Debi, Michael, and Ron Nucci for unexpected material. And to Ray Higgs for his uncompro-mising integrity, his unfailing encouragement, and his fre-quent neck rubs.

Most of all, thanks to Barbara Large, to whom this book is dedicated.

AFTER WORDS

My intent for this book was to touch people, to inspire and encourage them to trust themselves. I hope its readers will engage with the learning process of writing and learn to validate their struggles with words on paper. I want this book to mirror my workshops and be as simple and effective.

I wanted to set up a dialogue between myself and the reader, as equals. The philosopher Martin Buber referred to it as an "I - Thou" approach to true communication.

Yet as this book approached its final form, I found myself dragging my feet. Looking at it harshly, judging....

The thread of rebelliousness running through my adventures, my reaction and overreaction to the grownup world of rules and regulations, and my lack of respect for conventional teaching — all have left me feeling exposed, naked. I've wanted to cover myself with explanations, justifications, and apologies because I came from the wrong side of the tracks (educationally speaking).

Ibsen, the Swedish playwright, said that writing means "to sit in judgment upon oneself." "And," added psychologist Theodor Reik, "to acquit oneself."

Obviously, my struggle to trust myself (and thereby gain acquittal) versus my desire to gain the approval of others is not to be easily resolved. Psychologist Carl Rogers said, "I think it's often very hard for me, as for other writers, to get close to myself when I start to write. It is so easy to be distracted by the possibility of saying things which will catch approval or will look good to colleagues or make a popular appeal."

I remember speaking before a luncheon meeting of professional writers and editors associated with the University of Washington. I'm always afraid that an educated audience wants intellectual, refined commentary rather than my usual irreverant, permissive approach. However, when a professor asked me a question about a recent, highly praised book, I blurted out that although I respected the author's contribution to the field, personally I'd found the book totally unreadable, so turgid and obscure that I hadn't finished it. I didn't have time to feel presumptuous because the head of the English Department sighed loudly and said, "Thank goodness! I'd thought it was just me."

"Have you acquitted yourself?" asked my editor.

This book, if it stimulates or challenges you, the reader, may be acquittal enough. I know that my work, written and verbal, will continue on the edge of risk, and I'll continue to seek the courage to say what I think, seek to practice what I teach.

A Dialogue

AMUSE: Give it up!

ME: What are you talking about?

AMUSE: This acquittal thing.

ME: I'd like to, but.... Have you any suggestions?

AMUSE: Sure. How about settling for I-quit-al?

ME: How's that?

AMUSE: Repeat after me. "I quit."

ME: Okay. I quit!

The End

NOTES

Chapter Three

1. Alvin Toffler, *The Third Wave* (New York: Bantam Books, 1981).

2. Albert Einstein. Source unattributable. From a clipping that a student brought to class.

3. Pearl Buck. This quote appeared in *Press Women* (a monthly publication of the American Federation of Press Women), in 1970 or 1971, with no source stated.

Chapter Six

1. Eric Hoffer, *Reflections on The Human Condition* (New York: Harper & Row, 1973).

2. R.D. Culler, *Skiffs and Schooners* (Camden, Maine: International Marine Publishing Company, 1974).

Chapter Seven

1. Gustave Flaubert. Source unattributable. From a writer's magazine clipping that a student brought to class.

2. George Sheehan, M.D., *Running and Being* (New York: Warner Books, 1978).

Chapter Thirteen

1. C.G. Jung, *Modern Man in Search of A Soul* (New York: Harcourt Brace Jovanovich, 1933).

Chapter Fifteen

1. Calvin Coolidge. Source unattributable. From a MacDonald's (hamburgers) advertisement in a magazine.

2. Dorothea Brande, *Wake Up And Live* (New York: Simon & Schuster, 1936), p. 103.

3. Richard Bach, *Illusions* (New York: Delacorte Press, 1977), p. 92.

Chapter Seventeen

1. Rudolph Flesch, *How to Make Sense* (New York: Harper, 1954).

Chapter Eighteen

1. Annie Dillard. Interview in *Harper's Magazine*, February 1974.

Chapter Twenty

1. Mark Harris, Preface to *Short Work of It: Selected Writing* (Pittsburgh: University of Pittsburgh Press, 1979).

Chapter Twenty-one

1. Annie Dillard, *Pilgrim at Tinker Creek* (New York: Harper & Row, 1974), p.31.

Chapter Twenty-four

1. *The New Yorker*, March 15, 1982.

BIBLIOGRAPHY

Blakeslee, T. *The Right Brain*. New York: Anchor Press/Doubleday, 1980.

Bradbury, R. *Zen and the Art of Writing*. Santa Barbara: Capra Press, 1973.

Brande, D. *Wake Up and Live*. New York: Simon and Schuster, 1936.

Buzan, T. *Use Both Sides of Your Brain*. New York: E.P. Dutton, 1976.

Dillard, A. *Pilgrim at Tinker Creek*. New York: Harper & Row, 1974.

Elbow, P. *Writing Without Teachers*. New York: Oxford University Press, 1975.

　　Writing With Power. New York: Oxford University Press, 1981.

Koberg, D., and Bagnall, J. *The Universal Traveler*. Los Gatos, CA: William Kaufmann, Inc., 1972.

Restak, R. *The Brain: The Last Frontier*. New York: Doubleday, 1979.

BOOKS TO IMPROVE YOUR LIFE

From Whatever Publishing

Work With Passion — How to Do What You Love For a Living by Nancy Anderson, career consultant. This book shows you how to discover what you really love in life — your passions — and, better yet, how to develop a career doing what you really love to do. This has been called *the* career book of the eighties! (Hardcover, $15.95)

Friends and Lovers — How to Create the Relationships You Want by Marc Allen. An upbeat, knowledgeable, and contemporary guide to living and working with people, containing the simple and valuable formula for resolving conflicts so that *everyone* wins. Learn how to apply techniques that will improve the quality of all your relationships. ($6.95)

Creative Visualization by Shakti Gawain. Simple, practical, powerful techniques for creating everything you want in life. So clear and effective you can't help but experience immediate benefits. Over 250,000 in print. ($6.95)

The Creative Visualization Workbook by Shakti Gawain. Takes you step-by-step through many of the most effective techniques for dramatically improving your life in the areas of relationships, work and career, prosperity, health and beauty, and more. ($9.95)

Prospering Woman by Ruth Ross, Ph.D. Shows you that it is every person's birthright to live a full and abundant life. Just as effective for men as for women. ($8.95)

Weight No More by Karen Darling. The popular book that presents the completely non-diet weight-loss system that has worked for thousands of women and men. ($5.95)

14 Days to a Wellness Lifestyle by Donald Ardell, Ph.D., one of the nation's leading wellness pioneers. This enjoyable book spells out an easy, effective, and *fun* program for achieving optimum health and well-being. ($10.95)

CASSETTES TO IMPROVE YOUR LIFE

Stress Reduction and Creative Meditations. Marc Allen guides you through a deeply relaxing, stress-reducing experience on the first side. Side two contains effective, creative meditations for health, abundance, and fulfilling relationships. With soothing background music by Jon Bernoff. ($10.95)

Creative Visualization. Shakti Gawain guides you through some of the most powerful and effective meditations and techniques from her book. ($10.95)

Prospering Naturally. Ruth Ross presents dynamic, effective tools for increasing your prosperity. ($10.95)

14 Days to a Wellness Lifestyle. Don Ardell proves that wellness can be fun as he takes you through the 14 steps of his program. ($11.95)

ORDERING INFORMATION

Include $1.50 for shipping and handling for first item, and $.50 for each additional item. Send check or money order to: Whatever Publishing, Inc., P.O. Box 137, Mill Valley, CA 94942. Or phone: (415) 388-2100. California residents add 6% sales tax.

Order toll free with your VISA or Mastercard: (800) 227-3900; in California: (800) 632-2122. (Orders only, please.)

Allow 2-4 weeks for delivery — and enjoy! Satisfaction is fully guaranteed.

Write for a free catalog of fine books, cassettes, and music for good living.